Heian Flow System

effective karate kata bunkai

J W Titchen

Martial Arts Publishing Limited

Copyright John Titchen 2007©

All rights reserved.

No part of this book may be reproduced by any means, nor transmitted, nor translated into any format, without the prior written permission of the author.

1st Edition 2007

(v1.2)

Published by
Martial Arts Publishing Limited
www.MartialArtsPublishing.co.uk
email: enquiries@MartialArtsPublishing.co.uk

ISBN 0-9544466-2-3

Important Notice

The author, publishers, printers and distribution agents will not accept any responsibility for any proceedings or prosecutions brought or instituted against any person or body as a result of the use or misuse of any techniques or information described in this book or any loss, injury or damage caused thereby.

The information in this book is distributed without warranty and is only presented as a means of preserving a unique aspect of the heritage of the martial arts. All information and techniques are to be used entirely at the reader's discretion. While every precaution has been taken in the preparation of this book, neither the author nor publisher shall have any liability to any person or entity with respect to liability, loss or damage caused or alleged to be caused directly or indirectly by the contents of this book or by the procedures or processes described herein. There is no guarantee that the techniques described or shown in this book will be safe or effective in any self-defence, or otherwise. You may be injured or injure a 3rd party if you apply or train in the techniques described in this book. Specific self-defence responses illustrated in this book may not be justified in any particular situation in view of all of the circumstances or under applicable national, federal, state or local laws.

Dedicated
to
my parents and all my teachers

Acknowledgments

Tony Cobley – for always being game to be 'beaten up' by experimental applications whenever we have met up and for acting as my Uke for the shots here.

Rick Clark – for his encouragement, advice, teachings on vital point strikes and manipulation, and most of all for his vision in creating ADK International and thus giving me access to the ideas and experience of high quality martial artists from multiple styles across the UK, Europe, America and Australia.

Bill Burgar – for his advice as a mentor in the ADK grading process, his support and objective criticism in reading drafts of this text and for the excellent example put forward by his detailed study of Gojushiho.

Gerard O'Dea and **Steven Webster** – for their enthusiasm and encouragement and for giving me the inspiration to move from single technique application to flow drills. Drills 12 and 13 of this book have been taken with very little modification from a demonstration of their training methods at the Edinburgh University Shukokai Karate Club.

Susie Jayasinghe (nee Platt) – for introducing me to Karate, being such an excellent teacher and being mad enough to allow me and several other students to study Karate with her for 17 hours a week.

The Late John Tidder and **Alan Prescott** – for introducing me to the beautiful art of Aikido, being so patient in teaching me to relax and being such good teachers.

My former students at my Shiro Jishi Kai Club and my present students at the Practical Karate Group – for teaching me better ways of explaining and developing Karate technique.

Adam Piper, Robert Kemplay, Josh Lloyd and Bill Burgar – for taking the photographs for this text.

The other martial artists too numerous to mention individually by name – to all the students and teachers who I have met over my years in training who have influenced my approach to training in numerous ways and to others who I have never met who have influenced me through books, articles and videos.

Table of Contents

Acknowledgments 5
Foreword by Rick Clark 11
Foreword by Bill Burgar 12
How to use this book 13
   Aim 13
   Effective technique 13
   Heian Flow System 14
   Solo kata training 15
Kata application and the Heian Flow System 17
Effective technique 19
   Habitual acts of violence (HAOV) 19
      Location of incidents leading to hospital visits 20
      Assaults: type of violence used 20
      Sites of injuries sustained 21
      Attackers 21
      Time 22
      The nature of the robbery 22
      The location of the robbery 22
      Victims of theft 22
      Firearms 23
      The nature of violent attacks 23
      Male on male, close quarters 24
      Offences against the person, male on female 28
      The most common wrist grips, male on female 28
   Multiplicity 31
   Predictable response 34
   Initiative 35
   Redundancy 36
   Vital points 37
   Unbalancing 43
   Adrenaline tolerant 44
   Low maintenance 45
   Transferable skills 45
      Strength and fitness 46
      Techniques 46

| **History** | 47 |

Heian Shodan 51
- The kata movements 51
- Training rationale 55
- Changes to the kata movement in the Heian Flow System . . . 56
- Heian Shodan drills 56
  - Drill 1 56
  - Drill 2 58
  - Drill 3 60
  - Drill 4 62
  - Drill 5 65
  - Drill 6 67
  - Drill 7 69
  - Drill 8 71
  - Drill 9 74
- Advanced points 77

Heian Nidan 79
- The kata movements 79
- Training rationale 83
- Changes to the kata movement in the Heian Flow System . . . 84
- Heian Nidan drills 84
  - Drill 10 84
  - Drill 11 88
  - Drill 12 91
  - Drill 13 95
  - Drill 14 98
  - Drill 15 100
- Advanced points 103

Heian Sandan 105
- The kata movements 105
- Training rationale 109
- Changes to the kata movement in the Heian Flow System . . . 110
- Heian Sandan drills 110
  - Drill 16 110
  - Drill 17 113
  - Drill 18 116
  - Drill 19 119
  - Drill 20 123
  - Drill 21 128
  - Drill 22 130

  Drill 23 134
 Advanced points. 137

Heian Yondan 139
 The kata movements 139
 Training rationale 143
 Changes to the kata movement in the Heian Flow System 144
 Heian Yondan drills 144
  Drill 24 144
  Drill 25 148
  Drill 26 152
  Drill 27 156
  Drill 28 160
  Drill 29 163
  Drill 30 166
  Drill 31 172
  Drill 32 176
 Advanced points. 178

Heian Godan 179
 The kata movements 179
 Training rationale 183
 Changes to the kata movement in the Heian Flow System 183
 Heian Godan drills 184
  Drill 33 184
  Drill 34 187
  Drill 35 190
  Drill 36 196
  Drill 37 199
  Drill 38 201
 Advanced points. 204

Vital Point References. 205

Foreword by Rick Clark

Dr. John Titchen in *Heian Flow System* offers a unique perspective on the potential Bunkai and Oyo of the 5 Heian kata. Kata is an often underutilised aspect of training. This is due in large part to the misconceived notion that Kata does not offer any practical applications to real life situations. Dr. Titchen recognizes that human physiology dictates effective attacks will not vary cross generationally nor cross culturally. Simple assaults may involve nothing more than a shove or a grab followed by a punch. The predictability of such attacks allows martial arts to prepare defensive scenarios.

By preparing various scenarios of attack and defense it is possible for the individual to reduce the element of surprise of an aggressor. Surprise is a key element in both offensive and defensive techniques. Realistic training allows you to reduce the surprise you might experience in an actual attack, thus increasing your reaction time. By responding to such an assault in a quick and effective manner it is possible to gain a tactical advantage over your opponent and potentially turn the tables on them. This can only be done if training is realistic and employs effective counter techniques.

Dr. Titchen has done an admirable job of taking attacks listed in police records of the United Kingdom and relating them to the various movements found in the five Heian kata. In addition Dr. Titchen recognizes that martial arts training has become more and more popular in the world and the United Kingdom and demonstrates techniques that would be highly effective against individuals who have had basic martial arts training.

Dr. Titchen's current work adds to the body of knowledge of the martial arts and in particular to those who practice the Heian kata. I highly recommend to you this book, and encourage the reader to take the information presented here and apply it to your own particular martial art.

Rick Clark
Ao Denkou Kai
www.Ao-denkou-kai.org

Foreword by Bill Burgar

Over recent years the study of kata and the applications of kata has grown in popularity and many highly ranked karate-ka have taken up the in-depth study of this fascinating art. A growing body of work both in print and on DVD has become available. The majority of these have concentrated on individual techniques that each kata movement may represent.

Now more karate-ka are coming to understand that it is not enough to simply study individual isolated techniques but that each kata or series of kata should be seen as a whole self defense system. When viewed in this light the kata take on a whole new depth for those willing to study them and those karate-ka are always amply rewarded for their efforts.

John Titchen is one such karate-ka. He has taken time to study the Heian kata series in depth and has extracted not only applications for the movements but has also designed a set of two person drills that use those applications so that the karate-ka can practice with a partner in a controlled but aggressive environment.

All students of the Heian (Pinan) kata will find this book both interesting and useful in their study of karate. The information contained herein is not confined to the traditional kata, John has carefully researched the contemporary environment and applied the timeless lessons contained in the kata to the modern era.

I recommend the careful study of this work.

Bill Burgar
Author *Five Years, One Kata*

How to use this book

Aim

The aim of this book is to enable you to appreciate the Heian as not only a fighting system in its own right, but also a training system separated, for the convenience of both teacher and student, into five learning stages. The demonstrated drills illustrate not only how Kata can be brought to life, but also how they can play a major role in both self defence training (through teaching students how to defend against HAOV) and sport karate development (through teaching students at a very early stage how to move freely through a variety of ranges). Even if you do not train in the Heian/Pinan Kata, the illustration here of how to build upon the solo Kata training format with paired work, or simply how to string individual self defence drills together into a flow system, should prove highly beneficial to your own training regime.

In the Heian Flow System the techniques developed are designed for two different types of attackers:

1. An attacker who has had no prolonged martial arts training of any kind. This type of attacker is likely to attack using the Habitual Acts of Violence that have been determined from police records of recorded assaults in the United Kingdom. Since this form of attack is the most likely to occur, the majority of the exercises in the Heian Flow System have been designed to train students to defend themselves accordingly.

2. An attacker who has had some form of martial arts training. In the later stages of the drills students are taught techniques to enable them to negate some of the more common basic martial arts techniques which do not necessarily come under the HAOV umbrella.

Effective technique

Preceding the actual discussion of the Heian Flow System there is a section of the book devoted to discussing various technical principles through which we should endeavour to constantly assess individual moves or drills to determine whether they are likely to make us more effective martial artists or not. The individual techniques that make up the Heian Flow System have been measured against the criteria listed in this section and have been designed to meet the majority. For those who wish to study the drills, but are not necessarily able in their own clubs to train in them on a regular basis, the Effective Technique section provides a useful measure through which they can assess their own training strategies.

Heian Flow System

In this book the Kata and Heian Flow System is split into the five separate sections in which it is customarily taught. Within each Kata section there are a further four distinct parts:

- A complete demonstration of one of the Shotokan versions of the Kata.
- An outline of the learning processes encouraged by the Flow Drills designed around this particular stage of the Kata.
- A demonstration of the initial set teaching stages of the Flow System for that particular stage of the Kata.
- Suggestions and tips on how to not only increase the efficiency of the techniques in the drills demonstrated but also how these applications can either link with or act as redundancies for previously taught elements.

While there is no reason why the drills should not be introduced directly into a training syllabus with each grade immediately training according to their grading Kata, greater appreciation of the drills and Kata (and in turn greater ability to apply them) will come from having worked through the entire set as outlined in the following text. Although only the Shotokan form of the solo Kata is demonstrated, there is no reason why Karateka of different styles who use the Heian/Pinan in their training should not immediately be able to adapt to the Flow System set out here, or indeed use it with minor modifications according to their own method of Kata performance.

If you wish to use the drills as part of regular training in conjunction with the practice of the Heian Kata then my advice would be to teach the separate stages of the Heian Flow System prior to the solo form of the Kata they represent – this method tends to lead to a far greater level of visualisation during solo Kata training and consequently greater practical benefit to the student.

Solo kata training

The illustration of the Shotokan Karate Kata in this text is that of a set piece. This means that while the moves of the Kata are performed with the applications in mind, the entire Kata is executed from start to finish in one go. This form of training is appropriate for groups in the dojo but is not the most effective form of solo Kata training available. When practising Kata in your own time it is best to follow the pattern of your applications. As an example, my Kata training follows the order of the techniques of the Kata in which I am training, but each sequence will begin either from a fence or the mid or end game position I imagine myself to be in when I execute the techniques rather than the final position of the previous technique. The Kata I perform solo thus mirror images the flow drills I have created; sometimes moves are repeated several times in sequence as I imagine different combinations of arm or leg positions in my opponent or differing levels of effectiveness in my techniques.

In my mind the Heian is one Kata, and thus while I may perform each level in turn, depending upon my visualised opponent's behaviour I may freely move to the most appropriate part of another stage of the Kata before returning to the stage of origin for my next training scenario sequence. One of the advantages of this staggered form of Kata training is that not only is it more realistic (and thus hopefully more appropriate for self defence) but it also requires a smaller training area – approximately 2m by 1m – allowing you to train wherever you want. Once the basic skills of visualisation are gained, training in such a small space in an environment such as the living room or bedroom of a house allows the possibility of experimenting with different forms of distraction to concentrate your visualisation skills and provide a more realistic environment. Examples of this include:

- Training in dimmed lighting or the dark.
- Training with loud music in the background to distract your senses.
- Training with the television on to distract your eyes through movement.
- Training around furniture to restrict the ways you can move.
- Training in the garage to simulate the cold of the street.

Kata application and the Heian Flow System

The applications for the Kata demonstrated in the following pages are neither definitive nor exhaustive.

Many of the core techniques of the Heian set such as Upward Receiver, Down Sweep, Knife Hand Receiver and Augmented Inside Receiver have multiple applications not featured in the Heian Flow System and this wealth of potential technique is part of the reason why the Heian is so valuable.

The Kata is both a training tool and a fighting system in its own right. There is no reason why someone who only studied and drilled the Heian/Pinan kata in depth could not be as effective a fighter as one who only studied the Tekki/Naihanchi set or a single Kata such as Gojushiho or Niseishi. These Kata are each mnemonics that summarize the techniques and principles of fighting systems.

The applications for the Kata drilled in my classes are not exclusively those of the Flow System, those shown here as part of the Heian Flow System have been devised for the following reasons:

Taken together as a whole they provide students with effective defences against the majority of unarmed habitual acts of violence.

The applications have been chosen as they allow, in the majority of cases, free movement between techniques that either:

- follow directly from one another within the Kata, or
- are found within either that stage of the Heian or the Heian set as a whole.

The applications chosen thus teach students how to follow through if their original attack/counter-attack is ineffective and has failed to control or 'drop' the other person.

They progressively teach students in controlled situations how to react when their techniques are countered or blocked by a partner.

They teach students how to use the whole body as a weapon through appropriate co-ordinated movement of both upper and lower body and encourage freedom of movement between percussive and grappling techniques.

Effective technique

Habitual acts of violence (HAOV)

One of the most important factors that all martial arts training aimed at practical self-defence should address is its relevance to the habitual acts of violence (HAOV) common to its locale. The value of having acquired an excellent defence against all the front kicks to the chest or head that your training partners in the dojo attempt to connect with you is diminished by the fact that it is a form of attack you are unlikely to have to defend yourself against in a bar or on the street. Even in this martial arts film-fuelled age, most people don't use effective kicks until their victim is already lying prone on the ground.

The term HAOV is a commonly used derivative of a term introduced by Patrick McCarthy, HAPV - habitual acts of physical violence. Both terms are interchangeable but I prefer the use of HAOV since it accommodates certain actions that many would not regard as physical violence such as pre-fight physical posturing and verbal threats. These are the point where training and flinch responses and your own personal protection strategies should come into play - before the physical violence begins.

If our martial arts training is to have any validity from a self defence perspective then it must address the HAOV that we are likely to face in a conflict situation. It is important here to address the real situation and not media or film induced perceptions. While it is possible to gain a reasonable idea of pre-fight patterns in your locale by reading the brief assault descriptions (and police appeals for witnesses) in your local newspapers, the best sources overall (for the UK) are probably the statistics compiled by the Home Office. These are usually available through the easy access of the Internet and are updated on a regular basis. They do not solely rely on police evidence but are able to break down the country into local regions so that you can spot local crime and violence trends. In other countries crime patterns may vary according to local custom and the laws that govern the use and carrying of weapons, but accurate up to date statistics can usually be found through either enquiries at your local police office or by making searches on the Internet for police and government statistics.[1]

Every year new studies are published which reflect all known violent crime. There can be discrepancies between reality and report; much of domestic crime goes unreported and minor incidents involving bruising and chipped teeth may not be reported by either victim or location manager (in the case of a pub, bar or club) due to the wish to avoid future trouble or the fear of reprisals. The material presented here is the result of reading through several studies over a period of years. Although I have on occasion given precise percentage figures from individual reports, these have been chosen as they reflect a norm observed over several years and studies. Precise figures will vary from year to year, but the expected variance is so small that the conclusions drawn as to how they should affect martial arts practice should remain the same.

1 In the United States the US Department of Justice and the Federal Bureau of Investigation both provide advice and reliable statistical information. This may be accessed via the Internet.

Location of incidents leading to hospital visits

40% of all incidents occurred inside Licensed premises,[2] a further 20% took place just outside. Only 24% of the incidents recorded took place elsewhere in the street.[3] The British Crime Survey (BCS) of 2002/3 indicated that 29% of violent incidents overall (not necessarily alcohol related) occurred in the street, an increase on the precious year.[4] These statistics can be misleading. The most serious injuries recorded happened inside bars, pubs or clubs – not the most injuries. The most common site of all violent assaults is the street.[5] With regard to alcohol related incidents, approximately one third occurred within the bar/pub/club, one third just outside and almost a third elsewhere on the street; only a small proportion occurred at bus shelters or train stops.[6]

Assaults: type of violence used

The majority of attacks (46%) involved punches or kicks, while pushes accounted for 12%. Despite an apparent majority of incidents taking place inside (in alcohol related violence), only 10% involved the use of a bottle or a glass (and 1% a knife).[7] These figures are slightly misleading since they refer to the recorded end product of the event. The statistics do not show whether attacks involving punches and kicks were preceded by pushes. It is likely that punches tended to follow pushes while kicks tended to follow attacks that had already displaced the victim to the ground. According to the British Crime Survey punching or slapping occurred in 64% of incidents between strangers, grabbing/pushing in 43% (note the overlap percentage) and kicking in 24%. Incidentally these statistics suggest that you are more likely to be kicked by acquaintances (30% versus 24%) than strangers.[8] Glasses and bottles were the most frequently used sharp weapons in the night-time economy (accounting for 8% of facial injuries recorded in a national study of Accident and Emergency wards) and, though generally not fatal, cause the most disfiguring damage.[9] Sometimes attacks just happen, but often victims will have a conversation with their attacker (over spilt drinks, being jostled, looking at a girlfriend, mistaken identity, queue jumping at the bar) and this distraction tactic (or pre-fight mental preparation on the part of the attacker) needs to be anticipated.[10]

---

2   Areas such as restaurants, bars, hotels or nightclubs that are allowed to sell alcohol for consumption on their premises.
3   M. Maguire & H. Nettleton, *Home Office Research Study 265: Reducing alcohol-related violence and disorder - an evaluation of the 'TASC' project*, (March 2003), page 38.
4   C. Smith, J. Allen, *Violent Crime in England and Wales Home Office Online Report 18/04*, (2004), page 12.
5   See above.
6   M. Maguire & H. Nettleton, *Op. Cit.*, page 34.
7   See above, page 41.
8   T. Budd, *Alcohol related assault and the findings of the British Crime Survey*, (2003), page 17.
9   A. Finney, *Findings 214 Violence in the night-time economy: key findings from the research*, (2004), page 3.
10 Budd, *Op. Cit.*, pages 16 – 19.

Sites of injuries sustained

The majority of injuries sustained by casualties were to the Face/Neck/Head/Teeth (73%), while only 11% of injuries were to the Arms/Legs/Hands and only 3% to the Trunk.[11] According to later statistics in 2003/04 many of the less serious woundings (39% of violent crime) resulted in bruises, grazing and black eyes.[12] These injuries suggest attacks involving punches to the head and pushes resulting in falls to the ground hence the grazing). The group most at risk of violence overall was adult men aged 16-24 (15.5%) compared to women of the same age group (7.6%).[13]

Attackers

Alcohol-related incidents are more likely to involve multiple offenders than other incidents. Almost half of alcohol-related assaults between strangers involved more than one attacker. 38% of the incidents between acquaintances involved more than one person.[14] The majority of alcohol related assaults involve men. In the case of incidents involving strangers, 90% were men only, 5% involved women and 5% a mixed group. The majority of stranger related incidents concerned men aged 16-24 whereas incidents involving acquaintances were more likely to occur in the over 25 group. Approximately one third of alcohol related assaults involved someone the victim considered as a friend.[15]

In 2004/5 80% of violent incidents (comprising both alcohol related and non alcohol related events, stranger and known acquaintance assaults) were perpetrated by men, 13% by women and 7% by both sexes. This indicates that you should not assume that a group has no harmful intentions purely because it is of mixed sex. The under 16s made up 10% of attackers and the 16-24 group 48% (69% in the case of muggings). This age distribution shows no statistical change from previous studies.[16]

One element that we have to contend with from a self-defence viewpoint is a confrontation where physical assault is the by-product, rather than perhaps the sole intent, of an attack. The statistics above were taken from alcohol related assaults, but these only account for approximately 52% of all assaults. The percentage figures for single person attacks are skewed by the inclusion of all domestic violence (which is almost exclusively one on one) – the actual proportionate figures of street/bar assault involving more than one person are consequently higher. But since alcohol related violence only reflects half of recorded violent crime we should consider the available data on robberies to gain a fuller picture.

---

11 Maguire & Nettleton, *Op. Cit.*, page 42.
12 T. Dodd, S. Nicholas, D. Povey & A.Walker, *Crime in England and Wales 2003/2004*, (July 2004), page 67.
13 See above, page 78.
14 In the 1999 survey detailed by Tracey Budd's report into alcohol related assault 51% involved one offender, 17% two, 12% three, 21% four or more. Budd, *Op. Cit.*, Pages 15, 28.
15 Budd, *Op. Cit.*, page 15.
16 C. Smith, J. Allen, *Violent Crime in England and Wales Home Office Online Report 18/04*, (2004), page 12.

Time

Robberies are more likely to occur at night, although the likelihood of being robbed varies according to the age and sex of the victim. An example of this is that the elderly and young children are more likely to be targeted during the day, since they tend to be 'available' more at those times. According to the statistics, approximately half of all robberies occurred between 1800 and 0200 hours and half of all personal robberies took place at the weekend.[17]

The nature of the robbery

In a quarter of all cases (both men and women) the victim was physically attacked prior to any demands or robbery. Men were more likely to be confronted with a demand as the first point of contact than women (41% versus 25%), while women in turn were more likely to be subject to snatch attacks (37% versus 6%). Men were more likely than women to be engaged in conversation first as a con tactic to establish their vulnerability to robbery.[18]

The location of the robbery

We all know particular areas we believe to be vulnerable and thus try to avoid, such as dimly lit back streets or shadowy areas of civic parks. This tendency is not unknown to criminals. 50% of all robberies took place in the street against only 2% in subways, 4% in parks and 5% on footpaths.[19]

Victims of theft

A survey complied by Tricia Dodd, Sian Nicholas, David Povey and Alison Walker in July 2004 assessed the risk of theft from a person (as opposed to home or car burglaries).[20] In the time period of the study, based upon reported incidents, 1.4% of adults in England and Wales had been a victim of theft from a person in 2003/04. Of these incidents the group most targeted were women aged 16 – 24 (accounting for 3.3% of all thefts) and men aged 16-24 (2.5%). Theft from the middle aged and retirement aged groups of men consistently accounted for less than 1% of the reported crime whereas women aged over 25 in all the segmented age groups accounted each on average for 1.4% of thefts. It is clear from this that women are at greater risk than men overall, although young men have almost twice the risk of being robbed than any of the female age brackets over 25.[21] The targeting of youth suggests to me that it is the perception that they are more likely to have 'portable property' in the form of bank notes rather than credit cards and the latest technology devices for communication or personal entertainment on them.

---

17 J. Smith, *Home Office Research Study 254: The Nature of Personal Robbery*,(January 2003), page 33.
18 See above pages 39 – 43.
19 See above, page 38.
20 T. Dodd, S. Nicholas, D. Povey & A.Walker, *Crime in England and Wales 2003/2004*, (July 2004), pages 54 – 62.
21 See above, pages 54 – 62.

Firearms

At the time of writing in England and Wales the number of firearm offences per annum is gradually increasing. In the United Kingdom possession of firearms without a license is a criminal offence that will result in a jail sentence and licenses are generally issued only to those who use rifles for pest control (such as farmers) or a sporting activity within registered groups such as clay pigeon shooters. Access to the type of personal firearms which may be purchased and owned legally in other countries such as the United States is not possible through legitimate channels in the United Kingdom. In 2003/04 8% (68 fatalities) of all homicides in England and Wales were caused by firearms.[22] The total number of robberies involving firearms in the same period was 4030, representing only 4% of all robberies.[23] In England and Wales therefore the actual risk of being a victim of a firearm offence (though probably increased for those who work behind easily accessible cashier desks) is statistically small, given that (based upon reported crime) in 2003/04 only 1.4% of all people were robbed and of those robberies only 4% involved firearms. It is noteworthy however that the BCS of the subsequent year showed a 6% increase in firearm offences overall and a 32% increase in the violent use of firearms, but these are still less than half a percent of violent assaults overall.[24] The proportion of offences make it inappropriate therefore to tailor a high percentage of martial arts training to defenses against close quarter firearm attacks. In areas of the world where firearms are more prevalent statistics may differ and readers in those areas are encouraged to do their own research and decide for themselves the appropriate training ratio between armed and unarmed defences.

The nature of violent attacks

In 2001, in an article published in the Journal of the Shotokan Research Society International, R. J. Nash presented data that had been gathered from a Home Office study group formed to investigate violence within modern society, based upon evidence taken from Europe and the United Kingdom. This article listed, in frequency order, the most common pattern of attacks that were made on both men and women. These lists are reproduced here by the kind permission of Jeff Nash and the editor of the Journal of the Shotokan Research Society International, Bob McMahon. These lists tally with the types of injuries and statistics revealed by the earlier statistics and thus the attacks listed are worth considering.

---

22 See above, page 79.
23 See above.
24 S. Nicholas, D. Povey, A. Walker & C. Kershaw, *Crime in England and Wales 2004/2005*, (July 2005) page 81.

Male on male, close quarters

One person pushes, hands to chest,

which is normally followed by the pushee striking first, to the head.

A swinging punch to the head.

A front clothing grab, one handed,   followed by punch to the head.

A front clothing grab, one handed,   followed by punch to the head.

Effective technique

A front clothing grab, two hands,   followed by a head butt.

A front clothing grab, two hands,   followed by a knee to the groin.

| A bottle, glass, or ashtray to the head. | A lashing kick to groin/lower legs. | A broken bottle/glass jabbed to face. |

A slash with knife, most commonly a 3 to 4" lockblade knife or kitchen utility knife (apart from muggings, sexual assaults and gang violence, the hunting/combat type knife is seldom used).

A grappling style head lock.   A grappling style head lock.

Effective technique

Offences against the person, male on female

This data was gathered from interviews with victims and offenders and from statements. Data only covers robbery/sexual methodology and changes relative to first contact with victim ie., venue/ night/day etc.

Domestic violence is not covered as this is a specific subject of its own.

1. The victim was approached from the rear/side/front, a threat was made with a weapon, and then the weapon was hidden. Then the victim's right upper arm was held by the attacker's left hand and the victim was led away.

2. A silent or rushing approach was made from the victim's rear, and then a rear neck/head lock applied and the victim dragged away.

3. The same approach as in #2, with a rear waist grab. The victim was carried/dragged away, normally into bushes/alley etc.

4. The victim was pinned to a wall with a throat grab with the attacker's left hand. A weapon-shown threat was made, and then the weapon hidden, and the victim led away.

5. The victim was approached from rear/ front/side. The attacker grabbed the victim's hair with his left hand, and then she was dragged away.

The most common wrist grips, male on female

White here represents the male attacker and blue the female victim.

The attacker's left hand, thumb uppermost, gripping the victim's raised right wrist. The attacker threatens/ gesticulates with his right hand.

With the victim's right arm down, the attacker grips the victim's right upper arm with his left hand and her left wrist with his right hand.

The victim raises both arms, with both of her wrists gripped. The attacker's hands are vertical with the attacker's thumbs uppermost.

With the victim's arms down, the attacker grabs both upper arms.

With the victim's right arm down, the attacker's left hand grabs just below the right elbow, and his right hand grabs her wrist.

These studies are by no means exhaustive and I would recommend that anyone interested in this subject engage in further research of their own. What these studies can do is provide us with important information as to the nature of the attacks that we are likely to face. The techniques we choose to drill should be aimed at countering HAOV:

We should train predominantly to fight an attacker under the influence of alcohol. We must therefore expect a higher pain threshold and select techniques accordingly. We cannot rely on pain to stop an attack.

We should consider that attacks are as likely to occur in the confines of indoor spaces as outside and thus not rely on defences that require large leg movements.

We should train to expect 70% of the strikes to be aimed at head height.

We should expect to be grabbed or pushed prior to a physical blow.

We should expect to be attacked by a man in his physical prime.

We should expect approximately a 50% likelihood of being engaged by more than one assailant. Training in percussive techniques should take priority over locks. If your health allows - practice running.

Multiplicity

For a technique to be deemed effective it should have multiple applications. We should therefore be looking to drill techniques that fulfil at least one of the following criteria:

- The technique can be employed from a multiple of starting positions.
- The technique can be deployed against a multiple of attacks.
- The technique can be deployed pre-emptively in a multiple of ways.

Not all techniques fulfil all these criteria, indeed some very effective combat techniques may not even meet one, but those that do may give an important edge to our training. If a single trained movement can be employed to deflect or attack from a number of different positions then we can replace several techniques with one. Drilling in one technique as opposed to five has two distinct advantages:

- By spending more time on a single technique (and thus reinforcing the muscle, ligament and nerve control to a far greater extent) we can ensure that we have a defense that is faster, stronger and less requisite of conscious thought (more natural).
- Having a single response to a number of given stimuli rather than many means that there is less chance of a delaying mental log jam in the event of a situation developing.

Log jam is a term coined by Geoff Thompson and Peter Consterdine to describe the brain's reaction to an overload of information.[25] We have all heard the joke about the Karateka or Judoka who asked a mugger to give him time to put on his white suit, but there is a grave element of truth in the poor quality jest. Log jam refers to what happens when we have drilled in too many responses to the same situation: reaction time is slowed because the brain has to waste time selecting the most appropriate response.

A technique has greater use if it can be deployed from a number of different positions. Ideally we should be able to use a technique whether we have our hands at our sides, in front of our body in a fence, or even if we have been grabbed or are grappling with an assailant. The Fence is a term coined by Geoff Thompson to describe a range of inoffensive postures that aim to provide both protection and a degree of sensory information.[26] I mention here the physical postures although he examines mental fences and levels of attention in great detail. There are three types of fences that I would use:

Palms down "Submissive" Fence. Palms down "Submissive" Fence.

---

25   P. Consterdine, *Streetwise*, (Protection Publications, 1996), page 206.
26   G. Thompson, *Dear or Alive: The Choice is yours*, (Sumersdale, 1997), page 109.

Palms up "Exclamation" Fence. Palms up "Exclamation" Fence.

Invisible Fence. Invisible Fence.

I personally always prefer to adopt a staggered leg forward approach with all fences since I feel that this provides greater protection to my groin. In addition the positioning of one arm forward limits the probable ways in which your attacker may attempt grab or push you (of which more in the following section). The palm up or palm down position really depends upon the message you are trying to convey to your potential assailant about your intentions. The invisible fence should never be used when you are within punching range of a potential assailant.

Not every technique demonstrated in this text has multiple applications shown and not every technique demonstrates all the applications or variations that can be imagined or practically employed. What may become clear to the keen observer who analyses their basics is that the techniques that have the greatest number of different applications are the ones which occur in Kata with the greatest frequency. Coincidence? Unlikely. This could be due to two factors:

- We find the most applications for these because they are the techniques which due to their frequency and repetition in Kata we have become the most familiar.
- These techniques occur and are repeated in a number of different Kata because they are the techniques that the developers had the most applications for and as part of their training regime each repetition represented a different application.

Predictable response

Picture the following scenario: Martial arts practitioner A with 20 years of experience pairs up against B who has only two or three years of training. We would usually expect the former to have the edge. Why? A is likely to be considerably older than B and while we should therefore expect A's reactions to be either equal or slower, the speed of A's technique is likely to be slower than that of B. The answer to this question lies not so much in the physical capabilities of A as the more experienced practitioner, but in A's mental capabilities.

The key word in the previous sentence is experience. Through years of training A is likely to be able to accurately predict and counter B's moves in advance by reading (consciously or unconsciously) minute changes in B's posture and breathing. A is also likely to initiate some of these changes by setting traps for B with deliberate alterations in stance and posture. These changes allow A to predict what B is about to do and thus act rather than react.

We should consider the value of predictable response in according to two criteria:

- The foreknowledge of how we are likely to be attacked.
- The foreknowledge of how a body is likely to respond to our techniques.

A study of HAOV allows us to be forewarned about how we are likely to be attacked, but it is possible to go further than statistics. In a potential situation you should form a fence. Visualize your fence. How you position your body will limit the number of ways that an aggressor will feel safe in initiating contact. Consider whether you wish to face that person squarely or at an angle. Most martial artists are aware that this affects how they can attack, very few consider how it limits the attacks they are likely to face. Visualize your fence once again but now ensure that you have one leg and one arm forward and your body turned away slightly. Now consider the following:

- What is the attacker likely to grab/touch? Your forward or your rear arm?
- What is the attacker likely to push? Your forward or rear shoulder? Your chest?
- Which hand are they likely to punch with?

Your posture has already narrowed the probable methods of attack. It is important to recognize this and train with this in mind.

Foreknowledge of how a body is likely to respond to our techniques is even more important if we are to train effectively. When a sequence involving moves of more than one direction is practiced, consider how the other body will respond. When you hit someone, their body will usually either move away from the strike or fold over the striking limb. Does your follow up account for this? Do you practice the follow-ups you would have to use in the event of the body not moving as significantly as expected?

You should concentrate on techniques that maximize predictable responses from your opponent.

Initiative

In the training hall martial artists of most styles practice sparring at either medium or long range. It does not take long to become confident at these ranges... confident that you can evade any attack made.

This confidence is false and could get you killed.

Action beats reaction. The initiator always has an advantage. At long and medium range this advantage is negated somewhat by distance. It is the distance, not your reaction speed (however heightened this may be by years of training) that gives you the ability to react sufficiently to defend yourself. If you do not believe me I invite you to take part in a little experiment:

Stand so close to your partner that there is only one forearm length's distance between the two of you. This is 'kick off' range, the range where most fights take place.

Your partner is to attack you with one technique only, so put your arms loosely at your side as if you were engaging in one step sparring.

Now ask your partner to hit you wherever they like as hard as they can - your job is to try to stop them.

When you get up off the ground, ask if you can have a go too.

At 'Kick off' range the person who hits first is usually the one who wins the fight. Action beats reaction. You must be prepared to hit the moment you feel your fence has been broached or even sooner. I have hesitated to strike on two occasions; the first time I ended up being pinned down and punched and kicked on a bar room floor by a group, the second I was head-butted by the aggressor's accomplice on my blind side in a classic pincer movement. A large number of

Effective technique

techniques in this text initiate from either the fence or from a push/grab - I am not waiting for the punch.[27]

In English Law you are allowed to use reasonable force to defend yourself. This does not mean that you cannot strike first in self defense. If it was your honest belief that you were about to be attacked then you would be fully justified in striking first. Reasonable force is a variable - the bigger, more aggressive, more intoxicated your opponent the more reasonable a knockout or broken arm appears in order to prevent an attack.[28] Do not consider what is acceptable or not when in a fight. Do not consider anything other than creating an opportunity for escape. If you are busy worrying about what you can or cannot do your mind is not devoted to self-protection and that diversion could be fatal.

Take the initiative.

Keep the initiative.

Prioritize training in techniques that prevent the target from responding or escaping.

Redundancy

Self defence techniques should be designed to neutralise an attacker and allow us to escape as quickly as possible. It makes sense therefore to choose techniques that have a high level of redundancy.

Redundancy is a measure of how a technique can work if its original intent is not accomplished. A technique that can strike the opponent in a number of different ways depending upon range and position may be said to have a high level of redundancy since if the first movement does not have the desired effect the body is already compensating and moving without pause into a further attack. In similar vein a technique that both unbalances and strikes an opponent may also be said to have redundancy - even if the strike is not strong enough to end the conflict the unbalancing caused by the movement ensures that you still retain an advantage.

Redundant techniques should contain some of the following elements:

- Distraction: Visual/Aural/Physical (e.g. pain)
- Unbalancing
- Adaptability: the same movement can be applied at different effect at multiple ranges and angles
- Flow: the techniques can be trained to adapt to multiple outcomes
- Multiple Strikes (for example an uppercut that can become an elbow strike if the range is wrong)
- Targeting of Vital Points

---

27 I prefer the techniques that initiate from the fence and devote more time to training these. I strongly advise you to follow suit. In a public house do not assume that the barman will call for help - he may the best mate of the person picking on you. He may get into trouble with his employer if he calls the police.

28 Readers outside England should check the legal codes relating to their own areas.

Vital points

The following pages consist of diagrams showing some of the vital points on the human body labelled according to their meridian names in Traditional Chinese Medicine. Vulnerability to vital point strikes varies across the population: a small percentage of people have no reaction to vital point manipulation while an equal number are hyper sensitive, the majority of the population falls somewhere in between. This however is the experience of martial artists, in a dojo setting with sober students who are unlikely to have taken substances that affect the pain receptors in the body. With this in mind it makes sense to train to hit vital points, but not to expect them to have an effect on everyone. Thus we should target vital points with redundancy, where the target area will cause pain even if there is no response to the Traditional Chinese Medicine point. It is nice to have icing on your cake, but it is important to have a cake to put icing on to begin with.

The following diagrams are by no means exhaustive and show only the points targeted by my applications for the techniques demonstrated in this text. I have chosen not to highlight obvious target areas such as the eyes, neck, ribs, genitalia or kidneys. The following points have all been chosen because they have a high level of redundancy. A hard grab or strike to any of these areas will have an effect, even if you fail to strike the vital point correctly.

I do not intend in this text to give instruction on how to strike vital points. Anyone interested in the study of vital points for martial arts use should make further study. I have recommended three texts on this subject at the end of the text. I would advise anyone interested in training in the use of vital points to attend seminars on the subject.

Caution:

- The use of vital points can be extremely dangerous.
- Do not strike these points hard during training.
- Never strike any of the neck points during training - do not let anyone else strike your neck points.
- Do not practice vital point strikes unless there is someone trained in the relevant resuscitation techniques present.
- If you feel nauseous - stop training. If you continue to feel unwell, mentally or physically, seek immediate assistance from a qualified acupuncturist and inform them which points you have been working on. A General Practitioner of western medicine may not be able to help you.
- People taking drugs usually have a heightened reaction to vital point strikes.
- These points should not be practised on children or those of retirement age.

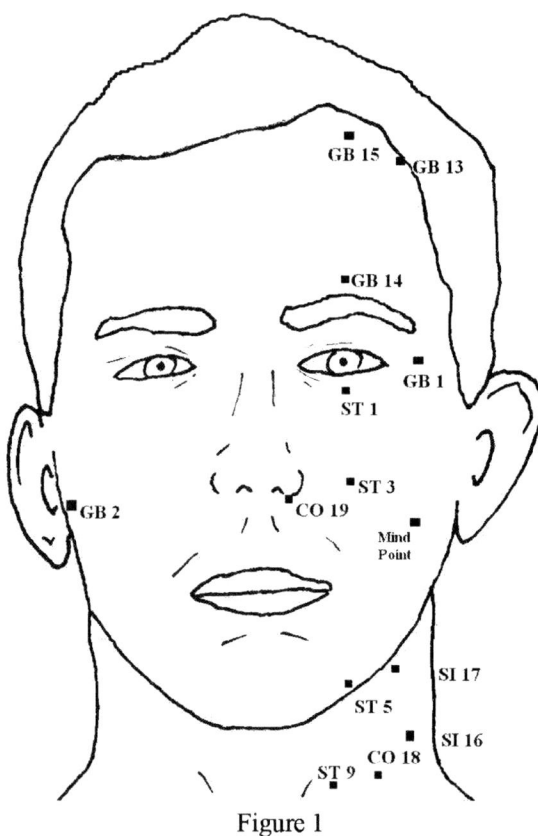

Figure 1

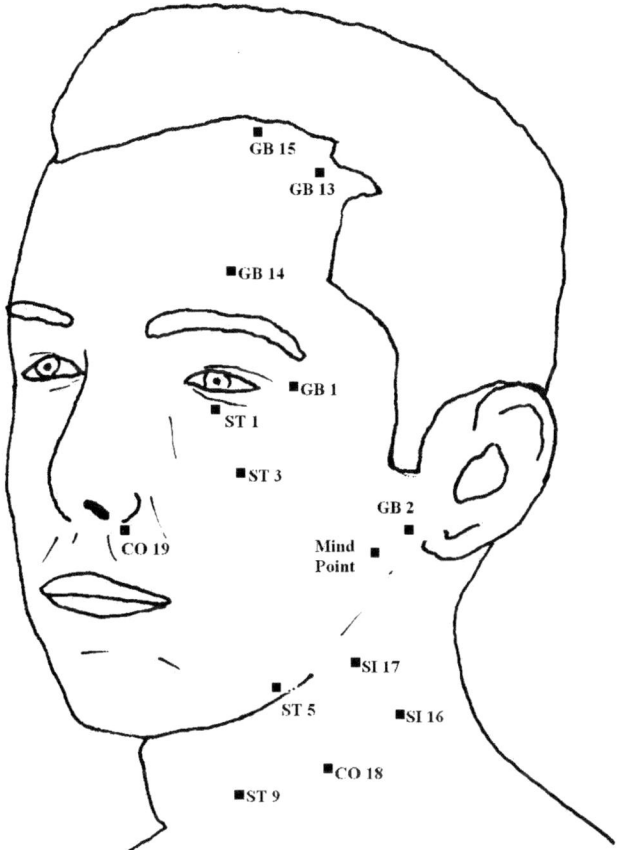

Figure 2

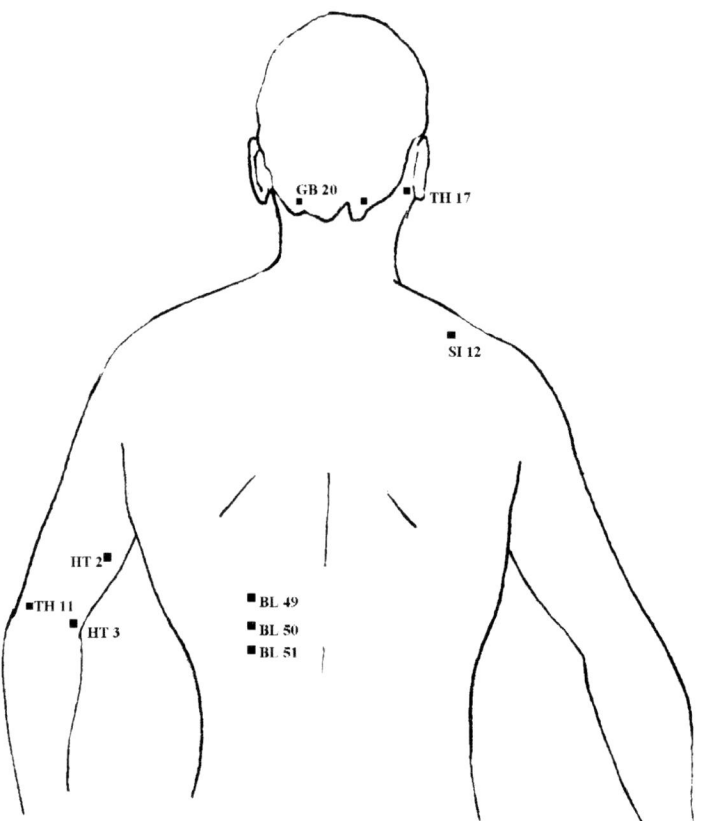

Figure 3

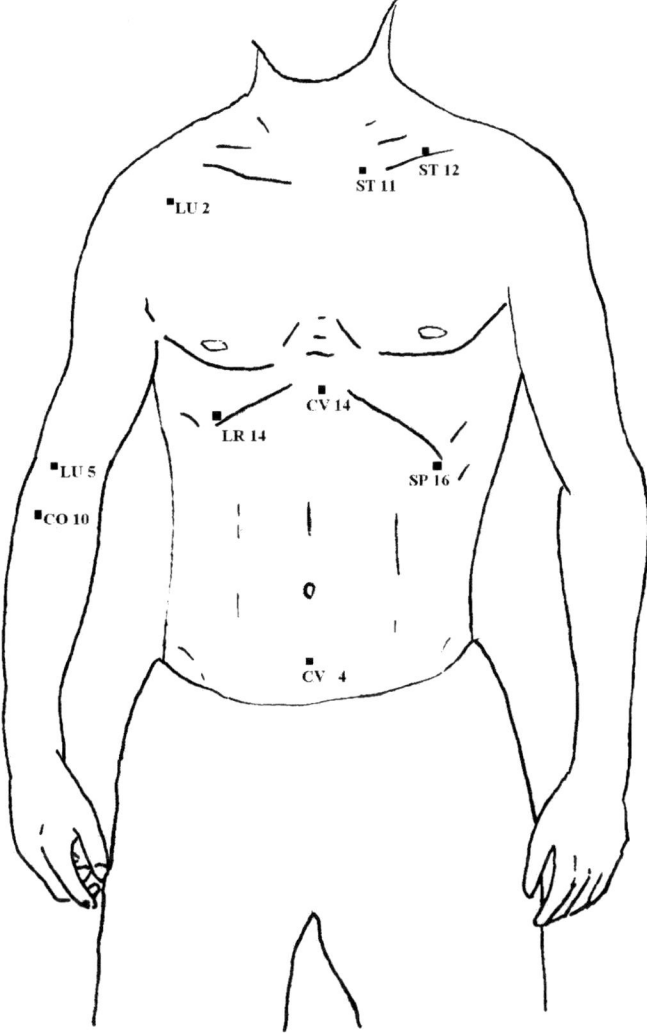

Figure 4

Effective technique

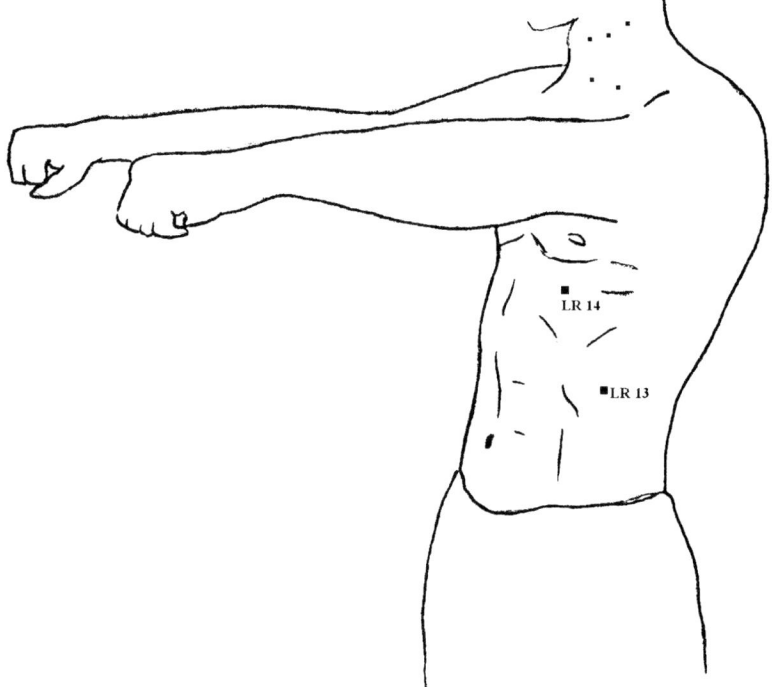

Figure 5

Effective technique

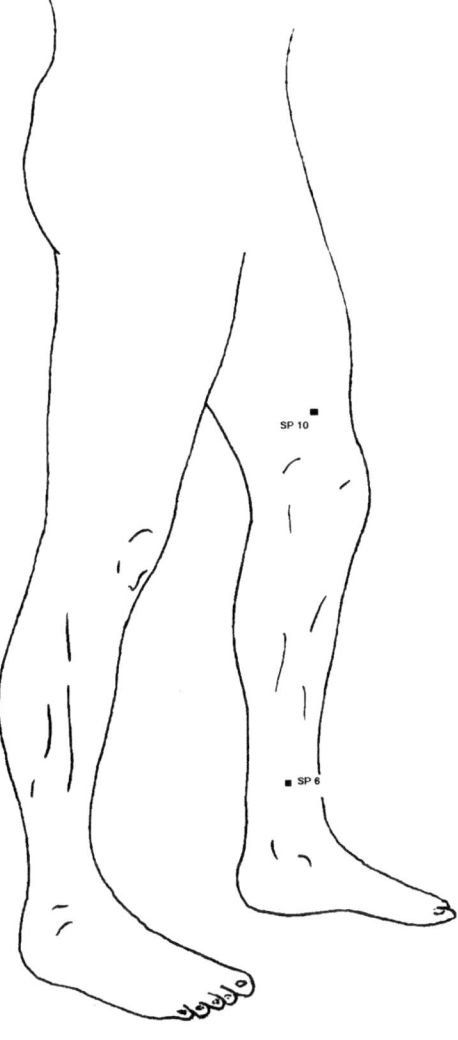

Figure 7

Unbalancing

This is such a simple concept that it is frequently ignored. It is not easy to concentrate or strike with power if your balance is taken. It should therefore be a priority in our choice of techniques that we drill techniques that distort an opponent's balance.

Many snub the tendency of some martial artists to practise the retraction of the hand to the hip. Such a technique has no use in the combat arena.

I don't think they could be more wrong.

I have no intention of punching from the hip, but I always practice pulling the hip and hand back together. Why? In my mind I am visualising that my hand has grabbed hold of something. It may be wrist, hand, sleeve, arm, lapel or even an ear. The development of the ability to pull an item rapidly towards you should be a priority. It transforms even the most mundane technique and increases its effectiveness by unbalancing your opponent precisely as you strike. The full withdrawal of the hand to the hip is an exaggeration, but one that serves the purpose of developing the correct pulling technique. In real life it is rare that the hand comes all the way back to the hip, but experience has shown me that training solo with a lesser motion does not produce the same results when applying the technique against a partner. Incidentally I do not advocate always withdrawing the hand to the hip – if it is unattached I frequently withdraw the hand to a guard position near the head.

The use of a grab and movement of an opponent's arm to either take the centre or to draw towards the third point are excellent tools in unbalancing, but to concentrate on these alone would be to ignore the extensive lower level repertoire that is available. The foot, ankle, knee and the major muscles of the leg are all particularly susceptible to lower level kicks or shunting attacks. These can be employed as an end unto themselves or to cause pain, distraction and lack of stability while a higher level attack is being employed by the arms.

- Unbalancing distracts your opponent.
- Unbalancing weakens your opponent's techniques.
- Unbalancing reduces muscle tension required to resist incoming punches.
- Unbalancing buys time.

Adrenaline tolerant

Many techniques that are easy to apply in the safe and predictable conditions of the dojo become difficult and dangerous in the conditions of a real fight (such as lack of space, the crowding of other people, poor light, excessive cold or heat, poor footing, excessive noise) due to the adrenaline released into the system. Adrenaline can distort our perceptions of events, affecting our vision, thought processes, co-ordination of movement, perception of pain and time. Techniques that require surgical precision and complex skills are most likely to be affected by adrenaline and thus we should aim to use those that predominantly only require gross motor skills and target areas are likely to have an effect even if the strike is not spot on.

It is important, where possible, to try and experience adrenaline release in a safe environment (such as in the dojo or on a theme park ride, not for example at the wheel of your own car on a public road driving far over the speed limit where with a small miscalculation you can endanger the lives of others in addition to yourself) on a fairly frequent basis. This is to allow you to become accustomed to what the release of adrenaline feels like. It is a unique sensation, probably slightly different for each of us, that can only too easily be confused with fear. To me the release of adrenaline feels for a moment as if two very cold eggs have been broken just inside the small of the back and the contents are flowing out. If your brain interprets the sensation of adrenaline release as fear then you become mentally at a disadvantage from the very beginning of any potential fight. Regular training that puts you under pressure, perhaps with some pre-fight posturing and shouting (and possibly in a darkened dojo in normal clothes), may stimulate adrenaline release and make you more accustomed to recognising it as a biological reaction that does not have to stop you from defending yourself.

Low maintenance

There are many excellent techniques that amaze audiences in cinemas world-wide. In this day and age some are created through the use of wires and technology, others by hours of sheer hard work on the part of actors, actresses, stunt performers and fight choreographers. We are often astounded by the ability of actors and actresses to perform these high-octane moves with such convincing panache. Would you be astounded to learn that by the time the movie is released most of the performers of these celluloid feats can barely execute a simple kick?

The reason for this is quite simple. Most of the moves which impress so much on the big screen are high maintenance. They require a degree of strength, flexibility, fine motor skills and timing that only a daily training regime of several hours can maintain. A further characteristic of such moves is that they require a degree of concentration that is extremely difficult (if not impossible for all but the most exceptional martial artists) to maintain when under the mental and biological stresses that a real fight produces.

High maintenance techniques are thus unsuitable for those who would take a practical approach to self-defence. Instead we should be looking at developing a repertoire of low maintenance techniques.

Low maintenance techniques

- Require little movement.
- Are easy to remember.
- Can be used under stress and adrenaline.
- Require few fine motor skills.
- Require little practice to remain proficient.

Transferable skills

How many of the techniques that you practise overlap?

There is only so much time in the day available to each of us to practice our chosen martial art. It should be one of our aims to maximise that time so as to reap the most benefit. Is there a way of training so that in practising for one skill we benefit another? Do we have transferable skills?

Strength and fitness

How many of us supplement our martial arts training with weights or fitness training? Could the time at the gym be spent concurrently working our physical strength and martial arts technique? Training in low stances builds good leg strength. The practise of slow kicks in low stances on the spot focuses the entire body weight on one leg (the equivalent of pushing 160 kg with two legs) while simultaneously working the balance, flexibility, accuracy and control of a kick. Would the aerobic benefit of a session on the rowing machine or the treadmill benefit your technique as much as 5 minute of fartlek training (intermittent fast and slow sessions) of techniques on a punch bag or solo Kata practice?

Techniques

The greater the number of cross-overs between techniques in your chosen repertoire the more likely it is that by working one you may benefit another - transferring skills. For example the set-up movement for many Karate receiving techniques is identical, if you have an application for that set up and you drill it each time you work on a different receiving technique then you are automatically drilling it. For example I drill essentially the same initial movement for both Down Sweep and Knife Hand Receiver- the end movement I choose depends upon the visualised success of the initial shared movement.

History

It has been said that the Heian/Pinan Kata were the creation of Anko Itosu (1832 – 1916). The most common source of this idea is the writings of Gichin Funakoshi, one of Itosu's students, who said that "Itosu had a natural genius for Karate-Do. It is said that he created the five Heian Kata".[1] Although Gichin Funakoshi credits Itosu with the creation of the five stage form as we know it today, his greatest strength, according to Funakoshi, was actually his practice of the Tekki/Naihanchi forms.[2]

Fortunately we do not merely have the anecdotal asides of Funakoshi to rely upon in our search for the origins of the Heian/Pinan Kata. In fact there may be evidence suggesting that Itosu was not the originator of the five stage form. It is possible to question Itosu as their creator through a study of the prevalence of the Heian/Pinan kata in styles not descended from his students. Taking the excellent study of Okinawan Karate by Mark Bishop as a guide we can see that the form is studied in the following styles: Chubu Shorin Ryu, Matsubayashi Ryu, Shorin Ryu (Shaolin) and Ryukyu Shorin Ryu.[3] These styles are descended from Chotoku Kyan (1870 – 1945), not Anko Itosu.[4] This would suggest that the originator of the set is a teacher common to them both; Sokon Matsumura (c1809 – 1901).[5]

It is still possible though that Itosu created the forms and that Kyan, as a contemporary, would have been exposed to them and decided to use them as a teaching method for his own students. It is certainly not unusual for martial artists to borrow ideas and methods from their peers. Alternatively the set may have spread to other styles through their inclusion in the physical education syllabus of Okinawan school children in 1901 – though it is interesting that this did not bring it to Okinawan based styles such Goju Ryu.[6] These factors seem to balance the arguments against Itosu, so perhaps the problem could be examined from another angle: the careers and teachers of both Itosu and Matsumura.

Anko Itosu, a well-educated member of the gentry class, had a career as a scribe and practiced martial arts as a secondary occupation (taking up the teaching of karate as a full time occupation only for the last fifteen years of his life). According to Choki Motobu, Itosu began his study of Karate under Matsumura, but was disliked by his teacher for his slowness and thus left to study under Nagahama (whom Gichin Funakoshi believed had studied under Wai Shin Zan). Nagahama apparently only taught karate as a means of physical exercise and body building, a fact he confessed to Itosu on his death bed, urging his pupil to return to his former teacher, Matsumura, for further instruction.[7] According to Gichin Funakoshi, Itosu's methods

---

1 G. Funakoshi, *Karate-Do Nyumon*, trans. M. Hironishi, (Kodansha International, 1988), page 100.
2 See above, page 100.
3 M. Bishop, *Okinawan Karate: Teachers, styles and secret techniques*, (London, 1989), pages 62, 171 – 174.
4 See above, page 62.
5 See above, page 62.
6 See above, page 31.
7 H. Cook, *Shotokan Karate: A Precise History*, (Norwich, 2001), page 22.

of practice more closely related to a teacher called Gusukuma who had been taught by a shipwrecked sailor from Fuchou.[8] Bruce Clayton has recently suggested that Itosu may have also been part of Matsumura's bodyguard team (and if that were so I would have to consider him a professional fighter), but the evidence for this is far from conclusive.[9] Itosu's 'main' teacher, Sokon Matsumura, worked as a bodyguard from 1827 to three successive Okinawan Kings (Sho Ko (1804-1834), Sho Iku (1835-1847) and Sho Tai (1848 – 1879). Matsumura is known to have been a good scholar and had ability sufficient to become an official in the Ryukyuan government. Matsumura's teacher on Okinawa was 'Tode' (China Hand) Sakugawa, of whom we have little information other than his name, social status (gentry) and martial ability (few sources can agree on the dates of his life, but he was certainly active in the second half of the eighteenth century). Sokon Matsumura is known to have twice visited Fuchou and Satsuma as an envoy and while at Fuchou he is said to have studied under two military attaches, Ason and Iwah. It is said that he went to Peking and trained at the Shan P'u Ying (Camp of Skilful Fighters), entirely possible if he travelled to the city as a member of an Okinawan delegation.[10]

There is no recorded evidence to my knowledge of Itosu having travelled as widely as Matsumura during the course of his life even though he is known to have had more than one teacher. Matsumura's occupation (throughout his life he was a professional warrior) and direct experience of contemporary Chinese fighting methods (Matsumura seems to have gained his experience through professional martial arts teachers and military envoys whereas Itosu's teachers other than Matsumura seem to have been individuals with only amateur knowledge), make it far more likely that he and not Itosu, was the father of the Heian/Pinan Kata. Attribution of these to Itosu is based on the hearsay of two of his students (Gichin Funakoshi and Choshin Chibana's student Katsuya Miyahira) rather than any solid evidence.[11]

8 G. Funakoshi, *Karate-Do Kyohan*, trans. T. Ohshima, (Kodansha International, 1973), page 8.
9 Clayton's theory is based upon the number of martial artists (including many who subsequently went on to become renowned teachers following the abdication of Sho Tai) linked to Matsumura who all had jobs that put them in close proximity to the Okinawan royal family. I feel that this suggestion by Clayton as the reason for so many accomplished martial artists close to the king is more likely than simply coincidence or patronage, but given the degree of surviving evidence it can only remain a theory, M. Clayton, *Shotkan's Secret, The hidden truth behind Karate's fighting origins*, (Black Belt Communications LLC, 2004)
10 H. Cook, *Op. Cit.*, pages 16 – 20.
11 M. Bishop, *Op.Cit.*, page 99 and Funakoshi (footnote 1). Although Itosu left behind a document of 'ten teachings' and we also have a copy of his letter to the Prefectural Education Department (which can be found in translation in H. Cook, *Op. Cit.*, pages 24 – 25 and M. Bishop, *Op. Cit.*, pages 102 – 103) in neither does he take credit for innovation in any particular Kata. This is perhaps most striking in his letter promoting karate as an educational tool – a modern author would have highlighted the fact that they had created a special series of exercises aimed at school children. We can either assume that Itosu did not create the Heian (or at least in his own eyes did not consider the changes he made as worthy of being considered a new form of training) or that he was suitably modest about his own achievements while promoting the cause of Karate.

It is possible that Itosu made slight modifications to the form when he introduced it to elementary education in 1901,[12] and this innovation has been confused with invention.

It has been said many times that the Heian/Pinan Kata is derived from the Kata Kushanku (Kanku-Dai). It is true that as a whole, the two have many movements in common, but the simple process of analysing and counting the prevalence of the techniques in both forms is enough to establish that they are at the same time very different. For a clearer picture look at the excellent technique Morote Uchi Uke (assisted inside receiver), it is one of the most common techniques in Heian/Pinan after Gedan Barai (down sweep) and Shuto Uke (knife hand receiver), occurring nine times. It does not appear at all in Kushanku. The Heian/Pinan set uses Age Uke (upward receiver) five times, it is also conspicuous by its absence in Kushanku. There are other techniques unique to Heian/Pinan that do not appear in Kushanku and visa versa. This of course does not prove that Heian/Pinan was not derived from Kushanku, what it does tell us is that it certainly had another source in addition to Kushanku for its techniques. Kushanku has entire sequences that are found in Heian/Pinan, but then it also contains complete sequences that are found in Passai/Bassai Dai as do the Heian/Pinan. It is entirely possible that the overlaps between the Kata may mean that they share a common ancestor and each is faithful (to a degree) to a different descendant.

The root of the Heian/Pinan form has been attributed to a (now lost) Chinese form known as Chiang Nan. Chozo Nakama (a second generation student of Anko Itosu) believed that the Heian/Pinan form was a remodelled version of Chiang Nan and that Itosu had learnt this from a Chinese who lived on Okinawa, changing the name to make it easier to pronounce.[13] Chiang Nan or Channan seem, to a non-Chinese or Japanese speaker (who may add their own qualifications to the following), to be very similar to the Chinese Qin (Chin) – na. The two Chinese characters have many subtle meanings, but the first could be interpreted as capturing / controlling / seizing while the second could mean holding/forcing/gripping/inducing.[14] Combined they seem to suggest the martial arts principle 'to control and induce' – elements of the most basic training, and the most advanced. The possibility that the 'original' Channan form may be named after a principle rather than a person could mean that:

- It may have been part of a group of Kata in a particular system and as such was not named after its founder.
- It may have been so old that its founder was no longer known (or if it came from a monastic source was anonymous) and as such was referred to by its principles.

If Heian/Pinan is merely a staggered form of Chiang Nan, a Chinese Kata (with possibly some Okinawan influences), then Kushanku/Kanku Dai is possibly a relation in the form of Uncle, Cousin, or Nephew. We know that Kushanku is believed to have been named after a Chinese

---

12 At the Shuri jinjo Elementary School. M. Bishop, *Op. Cit.*, page 102.
13 M. Bishop, *Op. Cit.*, page 99. Certainly Itosu changing the name would seem to suggest that he was not its originator.
14 T. Leung, 'Kung Fu Talks: Qin-Na: to capture and induce' in *Combat Magazine*, (July 1993), pages 30 – 34.

known as Kusanku (also Kushanku or Koso Kun) who visited Okinawa in 1756 as part of the retinue of the Chinese envoy.[15]

There are some techniques in the Heian, absent in Kushanku, that are so effective and have so many applications, that it does not seem likely that they would have been rejected from the formation of the Kushanku unless that person also knew Jion, where the majority (but by no means all) of the missing techniques also lie (although there are some techniques that seem unique to the Pinan/Heian, thus the possibility that Chiang Nan is the older form cannot be entirely ruled out). We cannot thus determine for certain the era of the Chiang Nan form that was adapted by Itosu, but we can be reassured perhaps that some of its techniques have been practiced for over 250 years – suggesting that they have been seen by succeeding generations of martial artists as effective. It certainly seems unlikely that the Chiang Nan modified by Itosu was particularly modern in its then form when he began to adjust it. This suggests that this Kata could have been initially studied and revised by Sokon Matsumura rather than Anko Itosu (though it was Itosu who changed the name). It certainly seems unlikely that the wider travelled and more experienced Sokon Matsumura did not know the Chiang Nan form.

The question of who formed the Heian/Pinan Kata remains a multi layered puzzle. How do we define the formation of a Kata? It is likely that Itosu, probably not a speaker of Chinese given his difficulties with pronunciation (unlike Matsumura who as an envoy to China we would expect to have been a competent speaker), changed the name from Chiang Nan. It is also likely that he made alterations to simplify certain techniques and make them safer for practice (such as the use of the corkscrew punch). But do these changes really make a new Kata? Few experienced people would claim that Tekki Shodan is really a different Kata to Naihanchi Shodan. The introduction of the form to the physical education syllabus by Itosu does not necessarily mean that it was he who divided the single form into five teaching segments, something that could also have been done by his mentor Matsumura. One or two techniques may have been changed or repeated as the form was split (such as the three sequential punches, three sequential Age Uke (upward receiver) techniques, three sequential arm bars and three sequential Morote Uchi Uke (assisted inside receiver) and the last four techniques of Heian/Pinan Shodan and Nidan are most likely additions to smooth the end of the form (taking a common line that mimics earlier elements of the form and being very different in nature to the endings of Sandan, Yondan and Godan). It is up to the individual practitioner to decide whether these changes really constitute the creation of a new form. I suspect that of those reading this book the belief that the form is something truly different in its present incarnation will be in inverse proportion to the length of time they have spent actually studying (as opposed to practising) Karate.

---

15 H. Cook, *Op. Cit.*, page 9.

Heian Shodan

The kata movements

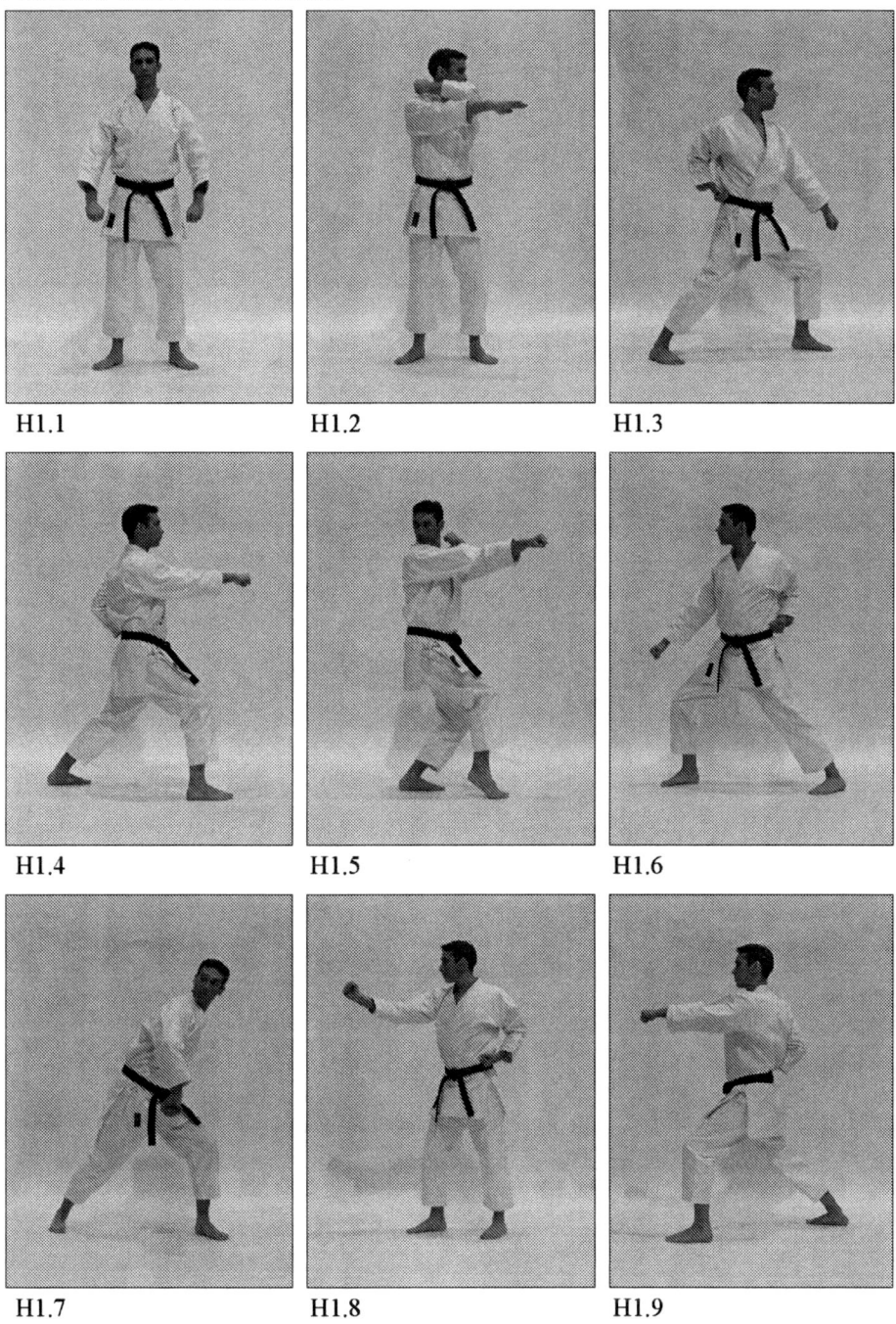

Heian Shodan

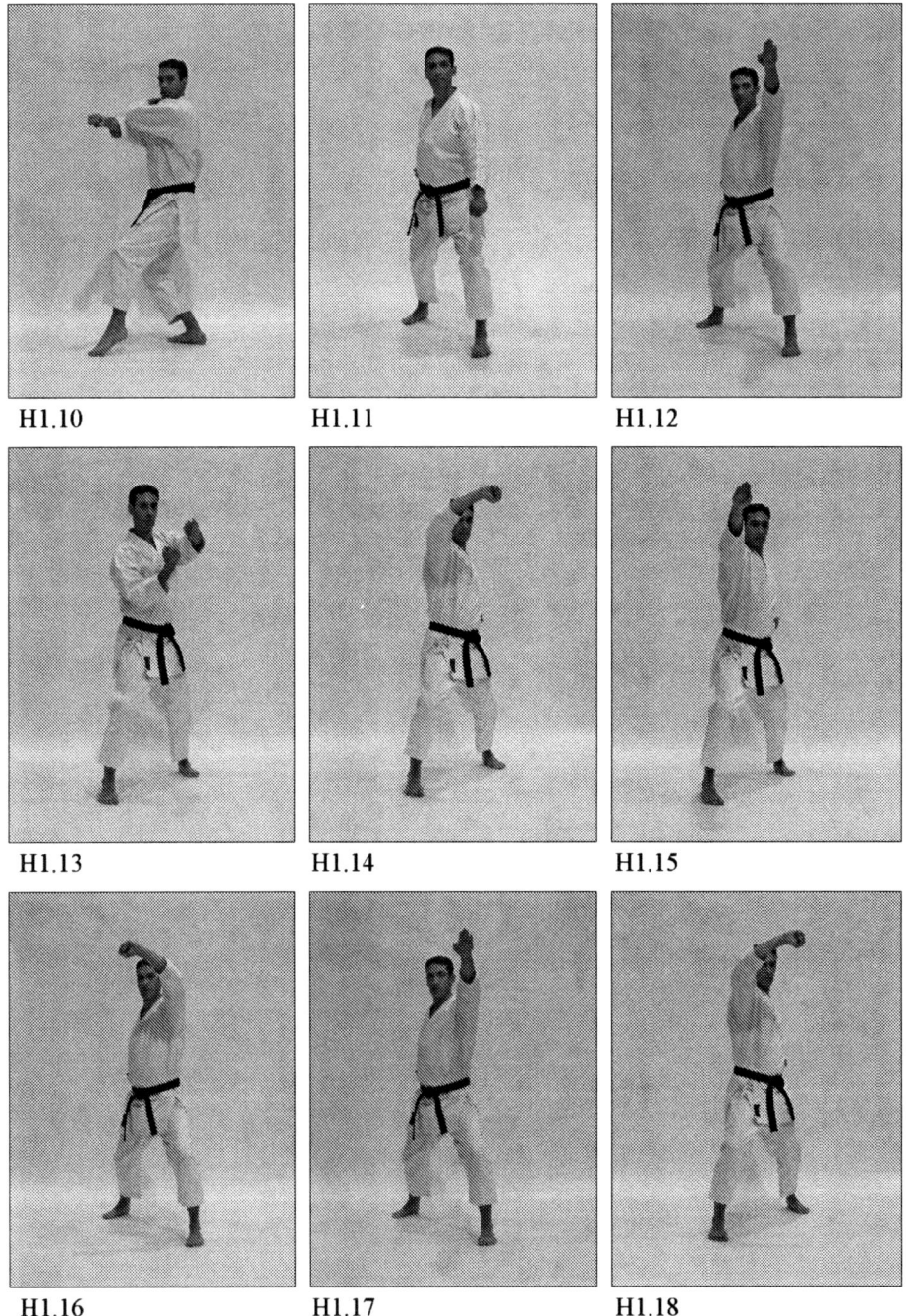

H1.10　　　　　H1.11　　　　　H1.12

H1.13　　　　　H1.14　　　　　H1.15

H1.16　　　　　H1.17　　　　　H1.18

Heian Shodan

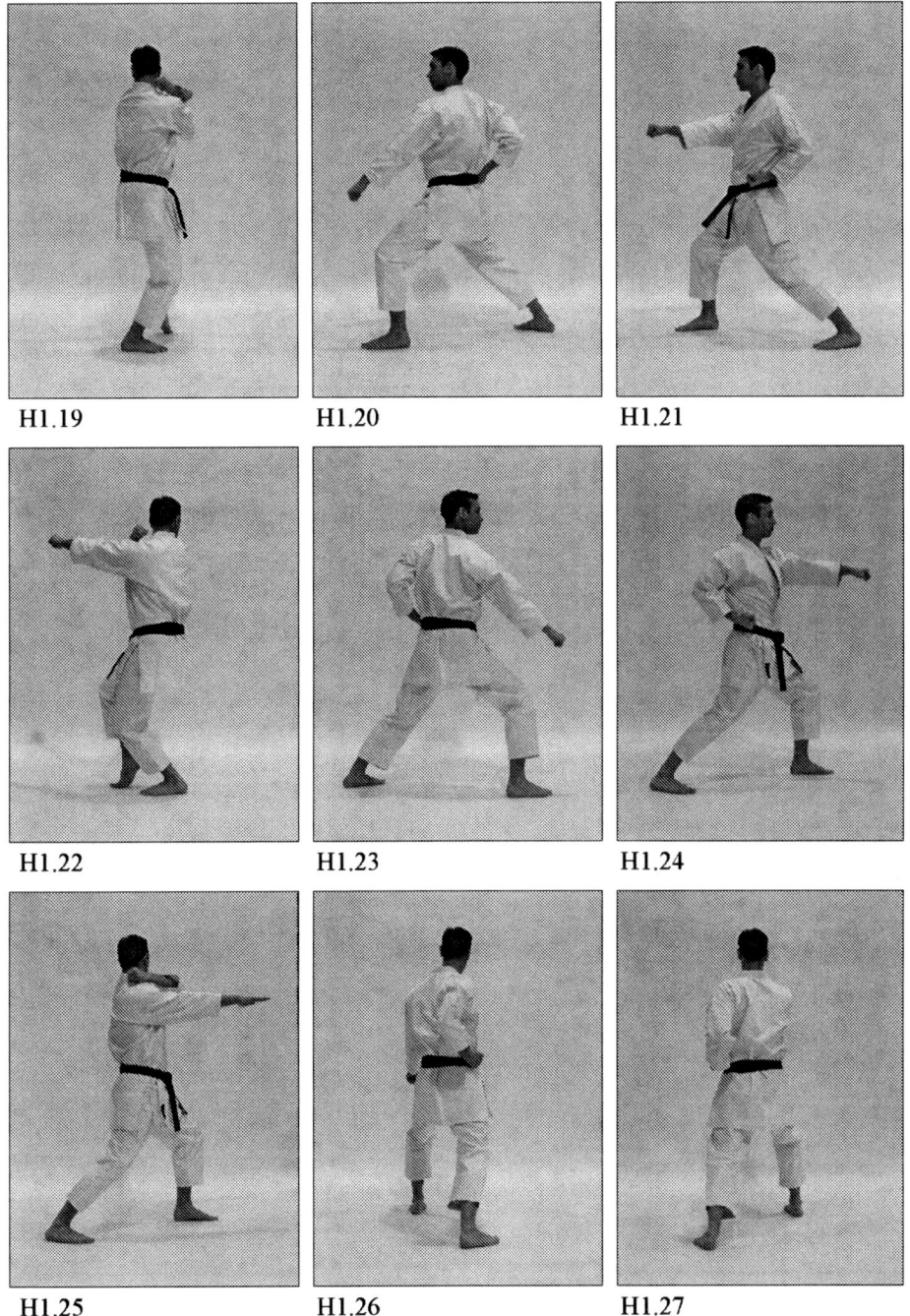

H1.19 H1.20 H1.21

H1.22 H1.23 H1.24

H1.25 H1.26 H1.27

Heian Shodan

H1.28　　　　H1.29　　　　H1.30

H1.31　　　　H1.32　　　　H1.33

H1.34　　　　H1.35　　　　H1.36

H1.37

Training rationale

In the Heian Flow system the order reversal of Heian/Pinan Shodan and Nidan imposed by Gichin Funakoshi has been kept. The reason for this is that while the techniques taught through the medium of Heian Shodan are no less effective than those of Heian Nidan, they require less initial training to gain a reasonable proficiency, rely on simpler movements overall and do not require an ability to kick with control and accuracy. Please note that all drills should be practiced on both sides, however students should give prominence to defending from their habitual fence. To ensure a level of realism and technique flow, when struck practitioners are asked to simulate a 50-70% successful blow, thus folding over in response to punches or head strikes but not dropping completely as per a knockout. This allows students to train to follow through naturally from one technique into another with a more realistic body position that is not provided by a purely rigid training partner. In many instances these people make a remarkable recovery midway through the drills, but this serves to keep both practitioners on their toes. The simulation of the body's reaction to actual strikes also teaches students about how the body is likely to move, serves as mental preparation for real events and improves visualisation skills.

The purpose of the Heian Shodan drills is as follows:

- To introduce students to paired training with a minimum of risk.
- To train students to maintain a fence.
- To train simple and natural flinch reflexes to intercept percussive attacks at medium and high level.
- To introduce students to the principle of unbalancing through:
  - Controlling/pulling an arm
  - Manipulating the third point
- To train students in simple but effective ballistic responses (including techniques with high redundancy)
- To accustom students to close quarter techniques such as shoves and pushes,
- To introduce students to defences against multiple punch combinations.

- To introduce strangulation techniques.

This is the simplest of all the drill sequences and interlinks only minimally with the subsequent drills. Its prime purpose is to simply develop an awareness of distance and a basic level of proficiency in intercepting percussive techniques.

Changes to the kata movement in the Heian Flow System

Sequences of movements are either initiated from a fence or a middle or end game fighting position instead of/in addition to the preceding movement in the Kata.

Heian Shodan drills

Drill 1

White and Blue face each other at medium range (Pic 1.1.1)

Pic 1.1.1   Pic 1.1.2   Pic 1.1.3
(H1.1)   (H1.3)   (H1.4)

White slides in with a low punch to Blue's abdomen. Blue counters with a flinch reflex forward arm down sweep and a 45 degree slide to the inside (Pic 1.1.2). Blue then grabs White's attacking arm and pulls as he steps in with a right punch to B's ribs (Pic 1.1.3). The forward knee should aim to target Sp 10 with the step.

Blue then shoves White away (Pic 1.1.4).

Heian Shodan

Pic 1.1.4

Effectiveness	Comment
HAOV	This is an uncommon initial attack. It is used here as an introduction and teaching technique to build a flinch reflex. The shove is far more common and its use here is to accustom the student to receiving the technique.
Multiplicity	The two techniques used score highly for multiplicity although here they are only being used in one way.
Predictable Response	This drill does not make great use of predictable response.
Initiative	The drill is reactive rather than proactive.
Redundancy	The punch may flow into Upward receiver as per Drill 3.
Vital Points	Potential Strikes to Co 10, LR 13, LR 14, CV 14, SP 10 and control via LU 7.

Effectiveness	Comment
Unbalancing	Unbalancing from below via a low level strike to SP 10 and potential unbalancing from above via pulling the arm downwards from LU7. Potential to unbalance via initial strike to CO 10.
Adrenaline Tolerant	Yes.
Low Maintenance	Extremely low maintenance.
Transferable skills	The stepping, unbalancing and striking skills are all used in other drills.

Drill 2

White grabs Blue's right wrist with his left hand (Pic 1.2.1).

Pic 1.2.1 (H1.6)   Pic 1.2.2 (H1.7)   Pic 1.2.3 (H1.8)

Blue pulls away from White, twisting his arm to break the grip (Pic 1.2.2) and counter-attacks with a right overhead strike (Pic 1.2.3). Blue follows through with a same arm strike to White's left arm (Pic 1.2.4) before grabbing it and pulling as he steps in with a punch to White's ribs (Pic 1.2.5). Blue then shoves White away (Pic 1.2.6).

Pic 1.2.4 (H1.3)   Pic 1.2.5 (H1.4)   Pic 1.2.6

Effectiveness	Comment
HAOV	This is the most common male on female wrist grip. The shove is common and its use here is to accustom the student to receiving the technique.
Multiplicity	Limited.
Predictable Response	This drill does not make good use of predictable response.
Initiative	The drill is reactive rather than proactive.
Redundancy	May progress directly into the punching attack if the wrist release fails.
Vital Points	Potential strikes to CO 10, LR 14, CV14, bridge of nose and control via LU 7.
Unbalancing	Potential to unbalance via strike to CO 10 and via pulling arm downwards from LU 7.
Adrenaline Tolerant	Yes.
Low Maintenance	Extremely low maintenance.

Heian Shodan

Effectiveness	Comment
Transferable skills	This drill reinforces a striking technique from Drill 1.

Drill 3

Blue and White face each other at medium range (Pic 1.3.1).

Pic 1.3.1

Pic 1.3.2
(H1.11)

White steps in with a low punch to Blue's abdomen. Blue counters with a flinch reflex forward arm down sweep and a 45 degree slide to the inside (Pic 1.3.2).

Blue then grabs White's attacking arm and pulls as he steps inside with a right upward receiver, moving fluidly from one strike into the next (beginning with either an uppercut or an upward elbow strike depending upon the range) (Pic 1.3.3 and Pic 1.3.4)

Blue then shoves White away (Pic 1.3.5).

Pic 1.3.3　　　　　　　Pic 1.3.4　　　　　　　Pic 1.3.5
(H1.13)　　　　　　　 (H1.14)

Effectiveness	Comment
HAOV	This is an uncommon initial attack. It is used here as an introduction and teaching technique to build a flinch reflex. The shove is far more common and its use here is to accustom the student to receiving the technique.
Multiplicity	The two techniques used score highly for multiplicity although here they are only being used in one way.
Predictable Response	The drill makes use of predictable response with the different elements of the upward receiver anticipating the probable body position of B through each level of the strike.
Initiative	The drill is reactive rather than proactive.
Redundancy	The upward receiver, consisting of several progressive strikes, has a high redundancy level.

Heian Shodan

Effectiveness	Comment
Vital Points	Potential strikes to CO 10, LR 13, LR 14, CV14, ST 9, CO 18, SI 16, ST 5, GB 2, ear, SP 10 and control via LU 7.
Unbalancing	Potential to unbalance via strike to CO 10 or ear and via pulling arm downwards from LU 7.
Adrenaline Tolerant	Yes.
Low Maintenance	Extremely low maintenance.
Transferable skills	Utilises techniques and skills developed in Drill 1.

Drill 4

Blue and White face each other at medium range (Pic 1.4.1).

Pic 1.4.1   Pic 1.4.2
(H1.26)

White steps in with a low punch to Blue's abdomen. Blue counters with a flinch reflex forward arm down sweep and a 45 degree slide to the inside (Pic 1.4.2).

Blue then grabs White's attacking arm and pulls as he steps inside with a triple punch combination of uppercuts (Pic 1.4.3, Pic 1.4.4, Pic 1.4.5).

Pic 1.4.3   Pic 1.4.4   Pic 1.4.5
(H1.27)   (H1.28)   (H1.29)

Pic 1.4.6

Blue then shoves White away (Pic 1.4.6).

Effectiveness	Comment
HAOV	This is an uncommon initial attack. It is used here as an introduction and teaching technique to build a flinch reflex. The shove is far more common and its use here is to accustom the student to receiving the technique.
Multiplicity	The techniques used here could be used from multiple positions in multiple situations.
Predictable Response	The drill reflects the probable physical response to effective low punching.
Initiative	The drill is reactive rather than proactive.
Redundancy	Any of the punches could easily adapt into Upward Receivers.
Vital Points	Potential strikes to CO 10, LR 13, LR 14, CV 14, SP 10.
Unbalancing	Potential to unbalance via low level strike with step into SP 10.
Adrenaline Tolerant	Yes.
Low Maintenance	Extremely low maintenance.
Transferable skills	Utilises skills and techniques developed in Drills 1 and 3.

Drill 5

Blue and White face each other at medium range (Pic 1.5.1).

Pic 1.5.1

Pic 1.5.2
(H1.31)

White steps in with a right haymaker to Blue's head. Blue stops this with a left interceptor and a covering right hand, twisting or sliding slightly to the inside of the punching circle (Pic 1.5.2).

Blue then grabs and pulls White's right arm and steps inside with a right knife hand receiver to the side of White's head/neck (Pic 1.5.3). Blue then shoves White away (Pic 1.5.4).

Pic 1.5.3
(H1.32)

Pic 1.5.4

Effectiveness	Comment
HAOV	This is one of the most common attacks recorded.
Multiplicity	The knife hand technique, though only used in one way here, has a high multiplicity level.
Predictable Response	The drill does not make use of predictable response.
Initiative	The drill is reactive rather than proactive.
Redundancy	Drill 12 shows the redundancy for this strike. Alternatively, if the strike is ineffective, the right forearm is well placed to execute a strangle in conjunction with the left hand.
Vital Points	Potential strikes to the bicep, LU 7, ST 9, CO 18, SI 16, ST 5, ear, GB 2, GB 1, SP 10 and control via CO 10.
Unbalancing	Potential to unbalance via low level stepping strike to SP 10 and from above with the strike to the ear and the gripping and pulling of CO 10.
Adrenaline Tolerant	Yes.
Low Maintenance	Extremely low maintenance.
Transferable skills	This technique is used extensively in subsequent drills.

Drill 6

Blue and White face each other at medium range (Pic 1.6.1).

Pic 1.6.1

Pic 1.6.2
(H1.14)

White steps in with a right haymaker to Blue's head. Blue stops this with a left interceptor (Pic 1.6.2).

Blue then grabs White's attacking arm and pulls as he steps forward to the outside of White's right leg with his own right and a right upward receiver sequence (Pic 1.6.3, Pic 1.6.4).

Pic 1.6.3
(H1.13)

Pic 1.6.4
(H1.14)

Continuing to grip White's right arm with his left hand, Blue pulls White's right arm downwards to take White's balance (Pic 1.6.5). Blue relaxes his right arm so that it lies folded across White's chest and pivots his hips and shoulders in a counter-clockwise direction, throwing White to the ground (Pic 1.6.6).

Pic 1.6.5
(H1.19)

Pic 1.6.6

Effectiveness	Comment
HAOV	This is one of the most common attacks recorded.
Multiplicity	The individual techniques that make up this drill have high multiplicity levels.
Predictable Response	This drill does not make use of predictable response.
Initiative	This drill is reactive rather than proactive.
Redundancy	Potential to flow into Drill 5 after initial interceptor. This drill trains eventualities where you are not able to shift to the inside of the punch.

Heian Shodan

Effectiveness	Comment
Vital Points	Potential strikes to the bicep, LR 13, LR 14, CV14, ST 9, CO 18, SI 16, ST 5, GB 2, GB 1, ear GB 32 and control via LU 7.
Unbalancing	Potential unbalancing via stepping strike to GB 32 and from above with the possible strike to the ear. Uses a throw.
Adrenaline Tolerant	Yes
Low Maintenance	Extremely low maintenance.
Transferable skills	Predominantly uses techniques developed in preceding drills.

Drill 7

Blue and White face each other at medium range (Pic 1.7.1).

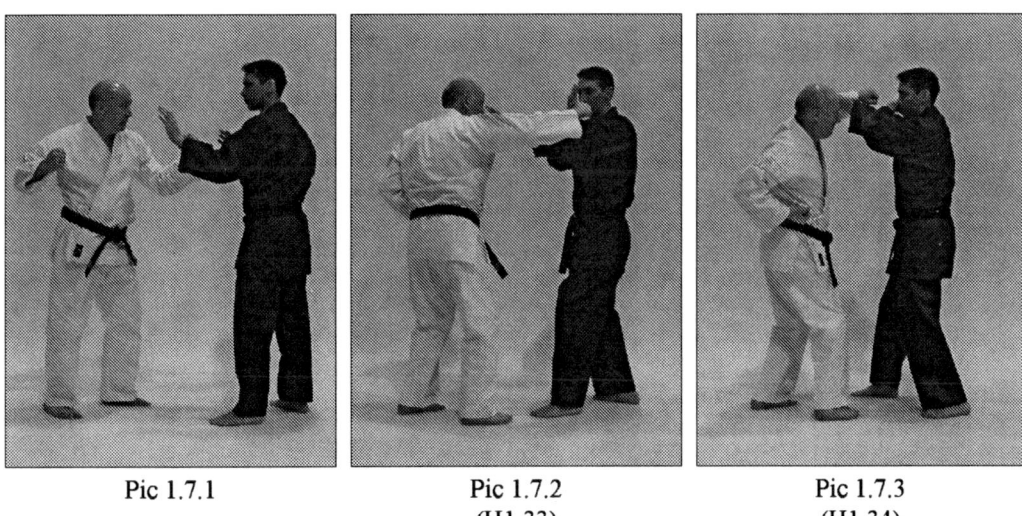

Pic 1.7.1   Pic 1.7.2   Pic 1.7.3
                   (H1.33)   (H1.34)

White steps in (or simply crosses on the spot) with a right haymaker to Blue's head. Blue stops this with a left interceptor and a covering right hand (Pic 1.7.2). As Blue is about to step into White with a right knife hand receiver White follows through with a left punch to Blue's head. Blue diverts his right hand strike to intercept White's punch, moving his right foot and hips to add greater stability and weight to his technique (Pic 1.7.3). Blue immediately follows through

Heian Shodan

with a stepping left knife hand receiver at 45 degrees to White's head/neck (Pic 1.7.4). Blue shoves White away (Pic 1.75).

Pic 1.7.4
(H1.36)

Pic 1.7.5

Note Blue should always attempt to land the knife hand receiver before the second punch is initiated, and White should try to make the second punch.

Effectiveness	Comment
HAOV	This is one of the most common attacks recorded.
Multiplicity	The knife hand technique is here used as both defence and strike and has many other possible applications giving it a high multiplicity level.
Predictable Response	This drill makes use of predictable response by training for the eventuality that the initial attack may be a common punching combination rather than just a single lunge.
Initiative	This drill is reactive rather than proactive.

Effectiveness	Comment
Redundancy	Potential to flow into Drill 12 after each knife hand receiver.
Vital Points	Potential strikes to the bicep, LU 7, ST 9, CO 18, SI 16, ST 5, GB 2, GB 1, ear, SP 10 and control via CO 10.
Unbalancing	Potential unbalancing from below by stepping strike into SP 10 and from above by pulling on the arm at CO 10 and the potential strike to the ear.
Adrenaline Tolerant	Yes.
Low Maintenance	Yes - the arms will automatically take care of themselves.
Transferable skills	This drill makes use of skills found in Drill 5 and many subsequent drills.

Drill 8

Blue and White face each other at medium range (Pic 1.8.1).

Pic 1.8.1　　　　Pic 1.8.2
(H1.31)

Heian Shodan

White steps in (or simply crosses on the spot) with a right haymaker to Blue's head. Blue stops this with a left interceptor and a covering right hand (Pic 1.8.2). As Blue is about to step into White with a right knife hand receiver White follows through with left uppercut to Blue's ribs. Blue diverts his right hand strike downwards to slap and strike White's left arm, dropping his weight backwards in a bent position to move his abdomen away from White's hand (Pic 1.8.3).

Pic 1.8.3
(H1.2)

Pic 1.8.4
(H1.2)

Blue immediately follows through with a low right punch into White's abdomen and a simultaneous rabbit punch or palm slap with his left hand to the back of White's head (Pic 1.8.4). Blue then drops his left elbow behind White's right shoulder and pulls while he simultaneously pushes with his right hand, turning White (Pic 1.8.5). Blue can then either strike to White's neck with the outer edge of his right thumb while elbowing White's right ear with his left elbow or strangle (Pic 1.8.6).

Heian Shodan

Pic 1.8.5
(H1.2)

Pic 1.8.6
(H1.3)

Note once both partners are proficient in this combination, B should give A no indication as to whether the attack is Drill 5, 7 or 8.

Effectiveness	**Comment**
HAOV	A single swinging punch is one of the most common attacks recorded. The punch uppercut is a variation on this.
Multiplicity	The knife hand technique is here used as both defence and strike and has many other possible applications giving it a high multiplicity level as has the down sweep that follows it in this variation.
Predictable Response	This drill makes use of predictable response by training for the eventuality that the initial attack may be a common punching combination rather than just a single lunge.
Initiative	This drill is reactive rather than proactive.
Redundancy	Potential to flow into Drill 12 after each knife hand receiver.

73

Effectiveness	Comment
Vital Points	Potential strikes to the bicep, LU 7, ST 9, CO 18, SI 16, ST 5, GB 2, GB 1, ear, SP 10 and control via CO 10.
Unbalancing	Potential unbalancing from below by stepping strike into SP 10 and from above by pulling on the arm at CO 10 and the potential strike to the ear.
Adrenaline Tolerant	Yes.
Low Maintenance	Yes.
Transferable skills	This drill makes use of skills found in Drill 5 and many subsequent drills.

Drill 9

White grabs hold of Blue's lapel or right biceps with his left hand (Pic 1.9.1).

Pic 1.9.1

White throws a right punch to Blue's head.

Blue shifts in slightly raising his left arm and striking White's right bicep with his elbow, raising his arm as if to smooth his hair. At the same time Blue punches White in the abdomen with his right hand (Pic 1.9.2).

Pic 1.9.2
(H1.2)

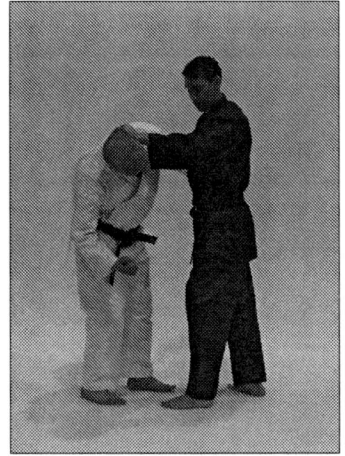
Pic 1.9.3
(H1.3)

Blue then hits across White's left temple with his right fist while pulling on White's left arm with his right (Pic 1.9.3). Blue then wraps his extended left hand round the back of White's neck and steps forward with his right leg, kneeing White in either the thigh or groin (Pic 1.9.4). As Blue steps down he pulls White's head towards him with his left hand and punches with his right (Pic 1.9.5).

Pic 1.9.4
(H1.4)

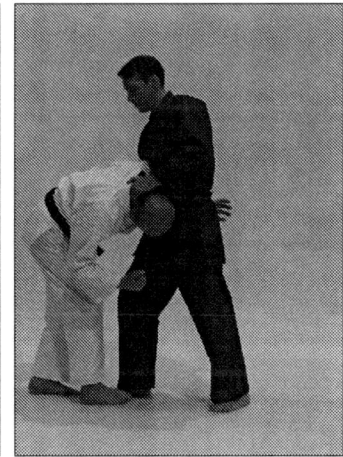
Pic 1.9.5
(H1.4)

Effectiveness	Comment
HAOV	This is one of the most common attacks recorded. Note the shortened range and the training for a missing fence.
Multiplicity	The down sweep technique is here used as both defence and strike and has many other possible applications giving it a high multiplicity level.
Predictable Response	This drill makes use of predictable response by training for the eventuality that the initial attack may be a common punching combination rather than just a single lunge.
Initiative	This sequence can be proactive and may be initiated without either the grab or the punch (in which case the angle of the elbow strike may change to the more common preparation position of the down sweep).
Redundancy	Multi level simultaneous strikes ensure that the chances of bringing down the attacker are high. The sequence has an inbuilt follow through in case the initial strikes do not stop the attacker.
Vital Points	Potential strikes to the bicep, HT 2, CV 4 - 14, ST 9, CO 18, SI 16, ST 5, GB 2, GB 1 and ear.
Unbalancing	Potential unbalancing from the spinning of the attacker's torso.
Adrenaline Tolerant	Yes.
Low Maintenance	Yes.
Transferable skills	This drill makes use of the techniques of Drill 1 in a short range setting.

Advanced points

As described above, the initial drills are at medium range to give students confidence. Once students are happy defending at this range the distance between partners should gradually be decreased to a more realistic level. Once this has been achieved B may attack on the spot with crosses for upper level attacks rather than stepping punches.

With training partner's consent all interceptor techniques should aim to strike either towards the face (as a distraction technique or attack depending upon distance) or to the top of the bicep at LU 4. The interceptor can strike directly into the armpit, but this is too painful for repeated practice and could be exceptionally dangerous.

When pulling a grabbed arm following a low punch, defenders should aim to take it towards the third point to destabilize their training partner more. Where possible the arm should be grabbed at Co 10 or LU 7.

When stepping inside an attacker, defenders should aim to drive their knee into SP 10. Conversely, when stepping outside GB 32 is a good target.

The covering hand during an intercept preceding a knife hand receiver could strike backwards into LU 7 (but in reality the fist should not be getting that close to your head).

Heian Nidan

The kata movements

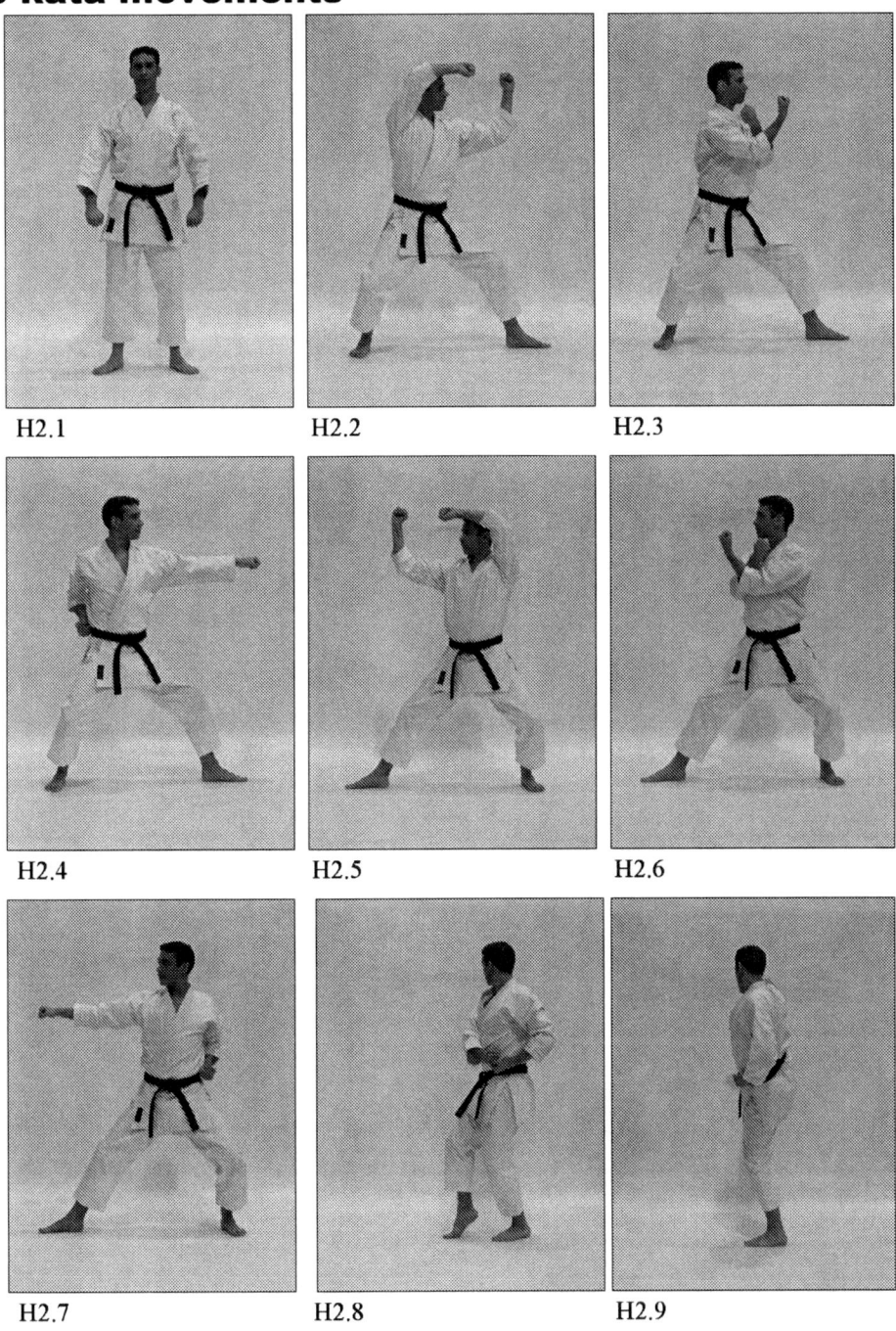

H2.1 H2.2 H2.3

H2.4 H2.5 H2.6

H2.7 H2.8 H2.9

Heian Nidan

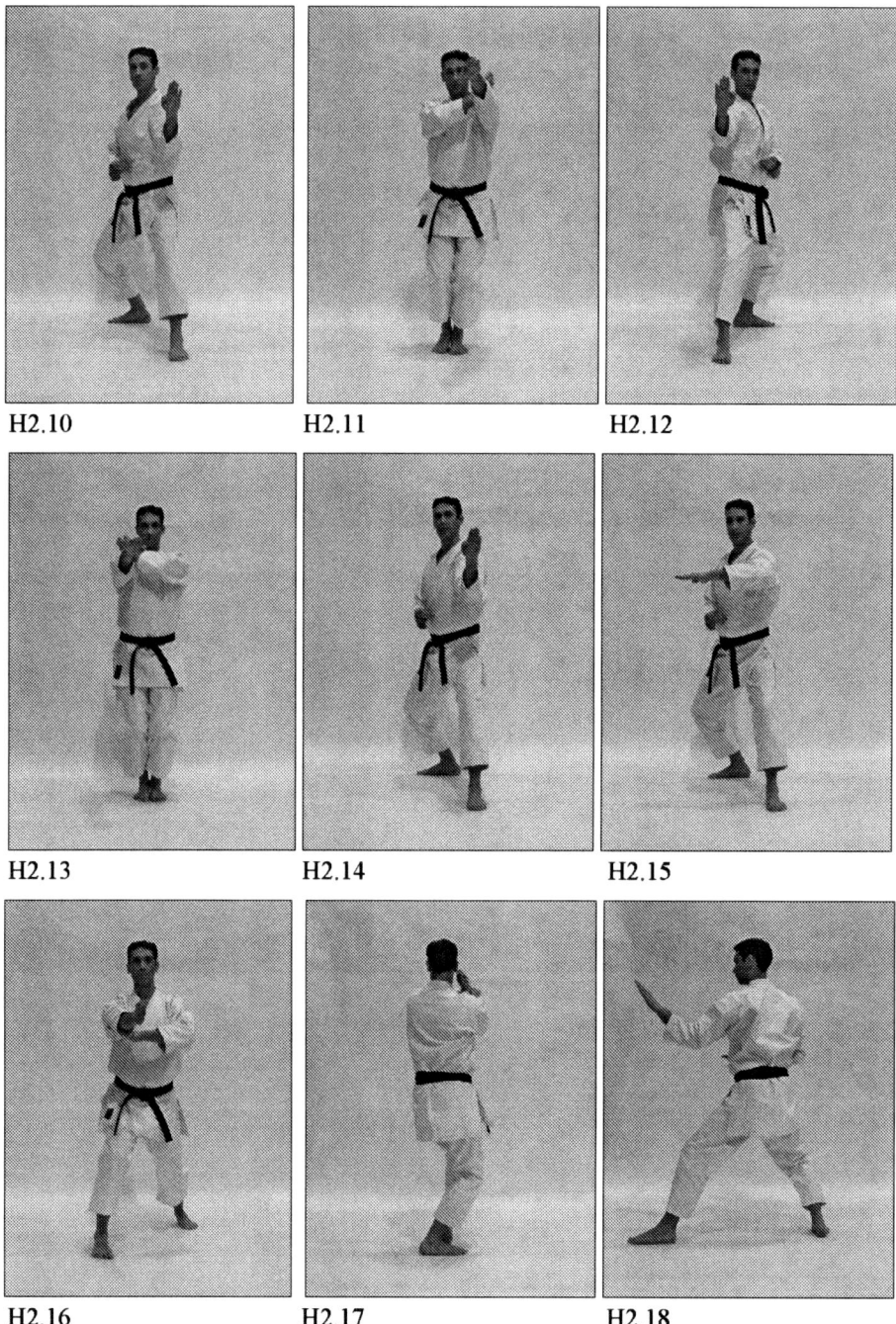

Heian Nidan

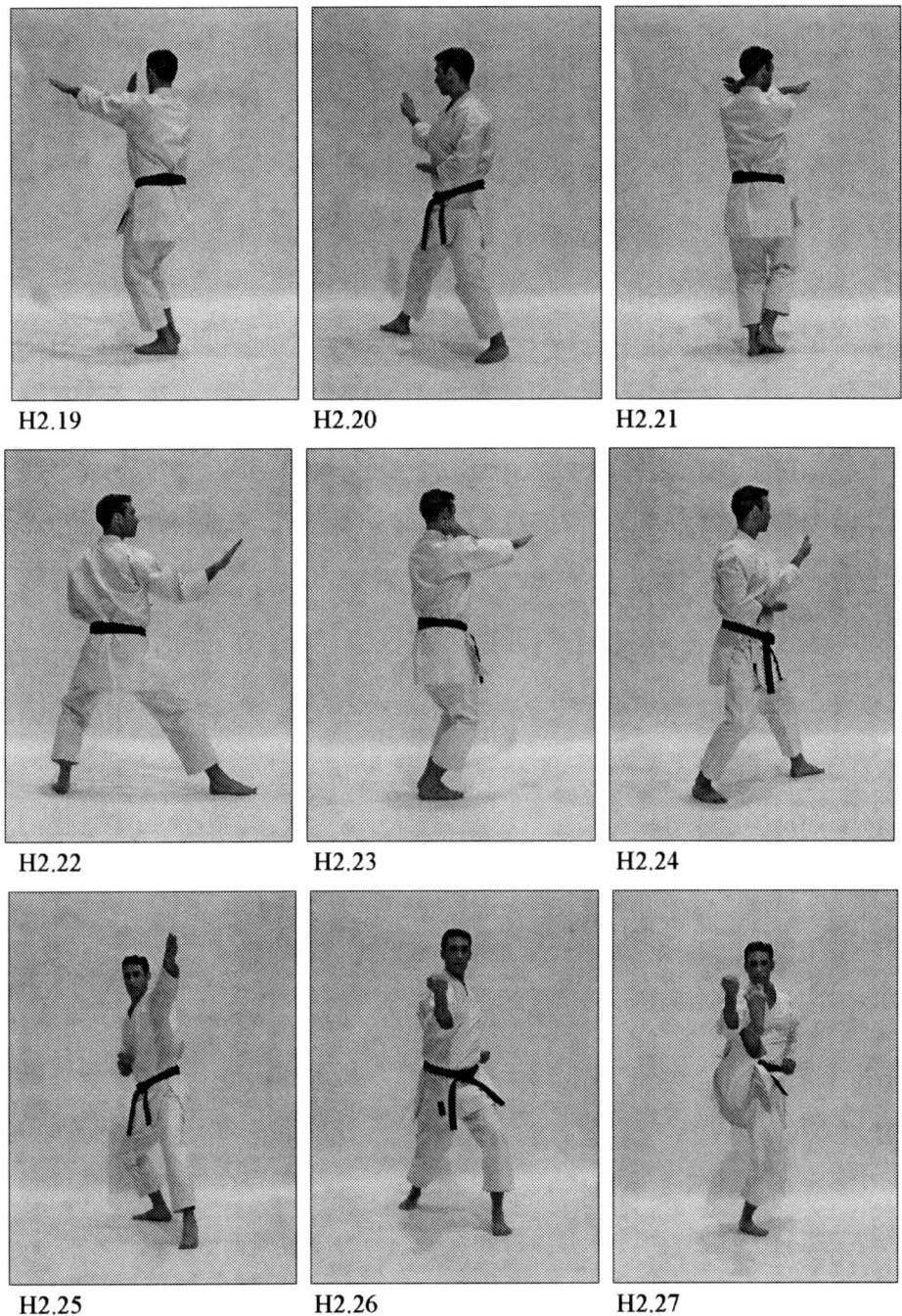

H2.19 H2.20 H2.21

H2.22 H2.23 H2.24

H2.25 H2.26 H2.27

Heian Nidan

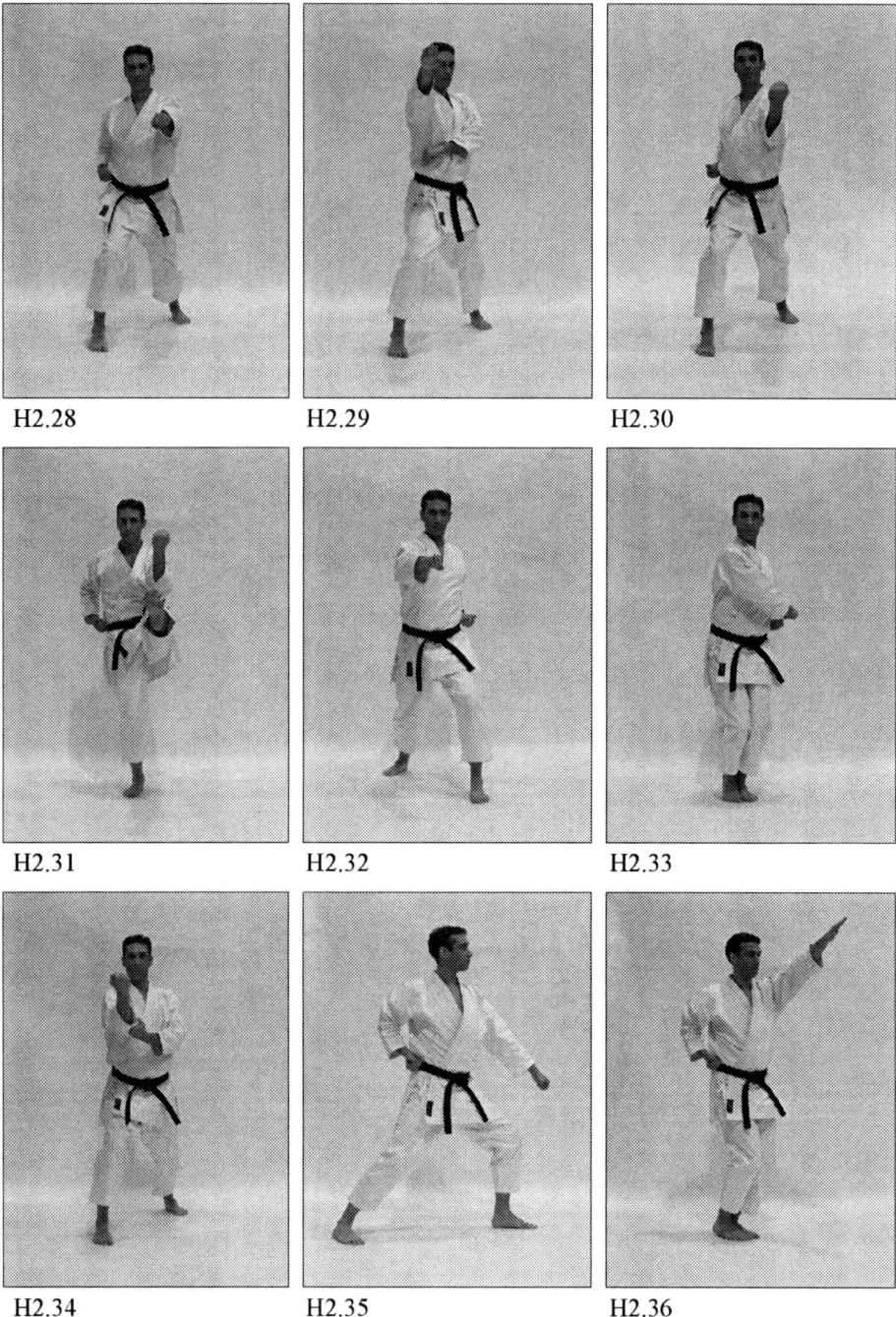

H2.28 H2.29 H2.30

H2.31 H2.32 H2.33

H2.34 H2.35 H2.36

Heian Nidan

H2.37　　　　　　　H2.38　　　　　　　H2.39

H2.40　　　　　　　H2.41　　　　　　　H2.42

Training rationale

Please note that all drills should be practiced on both sides, however students should give prominence to defending from their habitual fence. To ensure a level of realism and technique flow, when struck practitioners are asked to simulate a 50-70% successful blow, thus folding over in response to punches or head strikes but not dropping completely as per a knockout. This allows students to train to follow through naturally from one technique into another with a more realistic body position that is not provided by a purely rigid training partner. In many instances these people make a remarkable recovery midway through the drills, but this serves to keep both practitioners on their toes. The simulation of the body's reaction to actual strikes also teaches students about how the body is likely to move, serves as mental preparation for real events and improves visualisation skills.

The purpose of the Heian Nidan drills is as follows:

- To introduce students to moving with a partner to absorb energy and accustom them to responding to unbalancing techniques such as pulls.

- To work the concept of striking available targets such as the limbs to open further targets.
- To introduce students to the use of circular strikes and double arm strikes to exploit the weaknesses of tunnel vision.
- To reinforce the ballistic responses developed in previous drills.
- To introduce the use of kicking against both the abdomen and legs.
- To introduce an element of unpredictability in paired training.

Changes to the kata movement in the Heian Flow System

Sequences of movements are either initiated from a fence or a middle or end game fighting position instead of/ in addition to the preceding movement in the Kata.

In the opening mirror sequence of the Kata the line of movement is taken forwards rather than to the side since this allows an application of the technique appropriate to the training aims of this stage of the Flow System.

The side snap kick and backfist technique has been replaced by a knee strike followed by a front kick along with a straight punch which returns the technique more closely to the movement illustrated by Gichin Funakoshi in *Karate Jutsu*. The line of movement of this technique has been altered for the purpose of this application.

Heian Nidan drills

Drill 10

White seizes Blue's nearest lapel/arm or shoulder (Pic 2.10.1).

Pic 2.10.1   Pic 2.10.2
                    (H2.2)

White pulls Blue towards him as he throws a right cross to Blue's head (this can also be done with a step and pull with a haymaker). Blue steps forward with the pull with his right leg and pivots on the spot so that he is standing in a position similar to back stance, facing in the same direction as White with his weight predominantly on his right leg behind White. Blue uses the momentum of his step and White's pull to move him inside the circle of the punch which is deflected easily by Blue's left arm. At the same time Blue uses the momentum created by his hip pivot and change of direction to strike with his right fist to the back of White's head at GB (Pic 2.10.2).

Note the best angle to strike this area is upwards and inwards to the brain, the same angle created by the movement of Blue's arm (this lowered elbow position relative to that in many forms of the Kata also allows to shoulder joint to absorb a greater impact without injury). Practitioners should be aware of the dangers of striking the central spine C span in this way which could prove fatal. This should be a knockout blow, but for the purposes of the exercise White should simulate being stunned but not dropped.

The follow up has two variations:

1. Blue retracts his left arm to strike White's right ear with a reverse hammer fist while simultaneously his right fist punches White's left ear (this should create sufficient disturbance of White's ears to cause a complete lack of balance resulting in an inability to stand for several minutes) (Pic 2.10.3). In the event of an error Blue follows through by bringing his left hand to the left hand side of White's chin and then punching away from him into White's jaw (Pic 2.10.4).

Pic 2.10.3   Pic 2.10.4
(H2.3)   (H2.4)

2. Blue retracts his left arm to grab the top of White's head (striking with a cupped palm into the Gall Bladder triangle – GB 13, GB 14, GB 15) (Pic 2.10.5). At the same time Blue drops his right elbow and applies forward pressure with this (and his right forearm) to the back of White's left shoulder. As White pivots in response to the pressure, Blue's right hand reaches

Heian Nidan

up and grabs hold of White's chin from underneath (Pic 2.10.6). Blue now retracts his right arm sharply, pulling White's chin towards him while pushing away with his left arm (Pic 2.10.7). This variation should be exercised with extreme care in the dojo to avoid spinal injury.

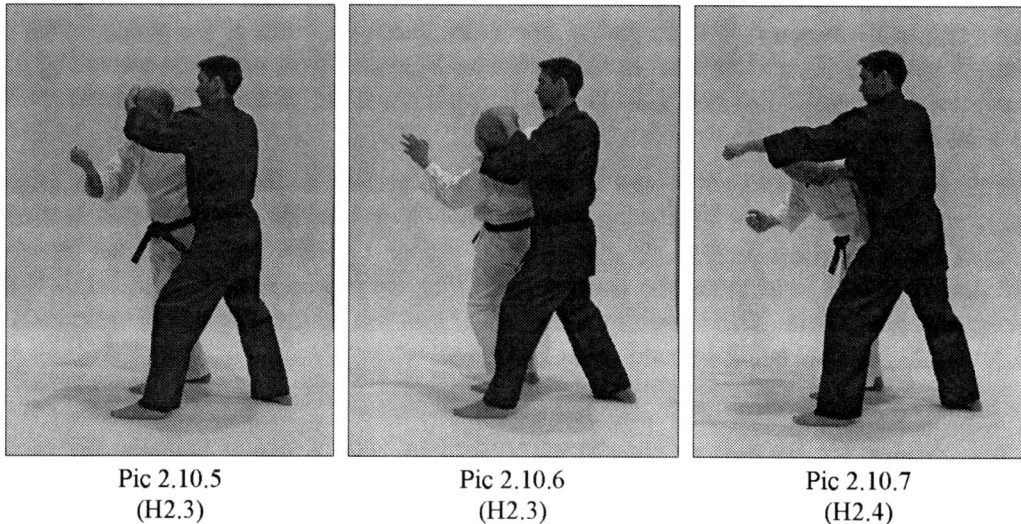

| Pic 2.10.5 | Pic 2.10.6 | Pic 2.10.7 |
| (H2.3) | (H2.3) | (H2.4) |

This technique forms the basic ingrained safety response in the Heian Flow System to any grab/punch combination that has not been dealt with pre-emptively before the punch has been thrown. It is best suited to a grab that pulls rather than a grab that pushes.

Effectiveness	**Comment**
HAOV	This is one of the most common recorded attacks.
Multiplicity	Low.

Effectiveness	Comment
Predictable Response	This technique makes use of predictable response. The forward shoulder/lapel/arm is the one likely to be grabbed and thus we can anticipate which hand is likely to punch and be prepared to move as a result. Thus the grab rather than the punch is the forewarner of the need for movement, this prior alert giving the stimulus necessary to avoid being hit at such close range. This drill also takes into account the likely physical forces at work such as the momentum of both the throwing of the punch and the pulling of the grabbing arm.
Initiative	This technique is reactive rather than proactive since the response is to the punch. Once the initiative is regained however it is kept.
Redundancy	The movements in this drill can be substituted by the original flinch responses of Drills 5, 6 and 7. After the strike to GB 20 in this drill the same movements can be used to two different effects.
Vital Points	Potential strikes to LU 7, GB 20, Mind point, Lu 5, ear, GB 13, GB 14, GB 15, CV 14 and LR 13 (by striking low rather than high).
Unbalancing	Potential unbalancing from above via strikes to the ears.
Adrenaline Tolerant	Moderate. The stepping movement will require regular practice – feet often glue to the ground under the influence of adrenaline.
Low Maintenance	No – requires regular practice but may be done solo to equal effect.

Effectiveness	Comment
Transferable skills	Develops the hip twist that adds power to strikes employed in back stance. The covering action of the left hand in its transitional stage mimics a standard covering guard used while employing jabs and crosses.

Drill 11

White grabs Blue's lowered right arm with his left while threatening with his right (Pic 2.11.1).

Blue relaxes his grabbed arm and slides alongside and almost behind White, pivoting so that he is facing the same direction. This motion brings Blue's grabbed wrist to his left hip, where his left hand can take hold of White's left wrist (Blue should turn his grabbed arm palm upwards – note in the picture the hand is forward of the hip for visibility) (Pic 2.11.2). Blue now lifts his knee to strike the thigh of White's nearest leg (Pic 2.11.3). Blue then extends his leg further to kick the back of White's left calf (Pic 2.11.4) before striking White's left temple with his freed right wrist while keeping hold of White's left wrist (note if White has not let go then the same movement with relaxed arms is likely to throw him) (Pic 2.11.5). If White then drops Blue simply steps back into a left fence. If White does not drop Blue can step back while striking outwards with a left knife hand receiver while his right arm controls White's left (Pic 2.11.6).

Pic 2.11.1
(H2.7)

Pic 2.11.2
(H2.8)

Pic 2.11.3
(H2.8)

Pic 2.11.4 (H2.9) Pic 2.11.5 (H2.9) Pic 2.11.6 (H2.10)

Effectiveness	Comment
HAOV	This is one of the most common grips used against females.
Multiplicity	This technique can be applied from avoiding a lunge or by side-stepping a push in addition to a grab.
Predictable Response	This technique makes use of predictable response by making use of knowledge of how the body responds to leg strikes.
Initiative	This drill is reactive but once the initiative is taken it is maintained through a blitz of strikes. The techniques can also be applied proactively with the practitioner's left hand grabbing the left wrist of the recipient.

Effectiveness	Comment
Redundancy	This technique has a high level of redundancy. It consists of a series of strikes, training the progression from one to another in the event of one not landing correctly. In addition there is ample opportunity to switch to a right knife hand receiver or upward receiver to attack the opponent once the range has been closed. An elbow strike can easily be inserted into the drill either in place of the backfist strike or prior to it.
Vital Points	Potential strikes to GB 32, BL 57, ST 3, CO 19, ST 5, GB 2, GB 1, ear and control at LU 7.
Unbalancing	Strikes to GB 32 and BL57 resulting in two 'dead legs' and subsequent unbalancing. Unbalancing from above via the following backfist technique to the face, especially if this connects with the ears.
Adrenaline Tolerant	Yes, The step taken is small and the initial knee strike is executed in a manner that cannot fail to strike the target and cause pain and balance disruption even if it does not hit GB 32. The follow through kick is harder to execute accurately and will require regular practice to be of use. The backfist strike at such range is easy to perform and works with instinct.
Low Maintenance	Yes. Easy to practise solo or paired.
Transferable skills	Increases situational awareness and works the skill of kicking accurately without having to look directly at the target.

Drill 12

Blue and White face each other in left fences (Pic 2.12.1).

White steps in (or simply crosses on the spot) with a right haymaker to Blue's head. Blue stops this with a left interceptor and a covering right hand (Pic 2.12.2). Blue then steps in with a right knife hand receiver to the side of White's head (note foot positions on this can vary, for added control the left leg can be pulled back as the right enters, adding power to both the strike and the pull) (Pic 2.12.3).

Pic 2.12.1   Pic 2.12.2   Pic 2.12.3
                      (H2.13)   (H2.14)

Blue the follows through by striking the top of White's left biceps with the blade of his right hand (Pics 2.12.4 and 2.12.5), before pushing his right elbow into White's sternum, shoving him backwards forcefully (Pic 2.12.6). Taking advantage of the distance gained Blue steps in with either a left palm strike to the side of White's jaw or a left spear hand strike (using the bent thumb as the attacking weapon) to the right hand side of White's neck (Pic 2.12.7) (note the right arm stays in place as a guard). (Pics 2.12.8, 2.12.9, 2.12.10, 2.12.11).

Heian Nidan

Pic 2.12.4
(H2.15)

Pic 2.12.5
(H2.15)

Pic 2.12.6
(H2.15)

Pic 2.12.7
(H2.16)

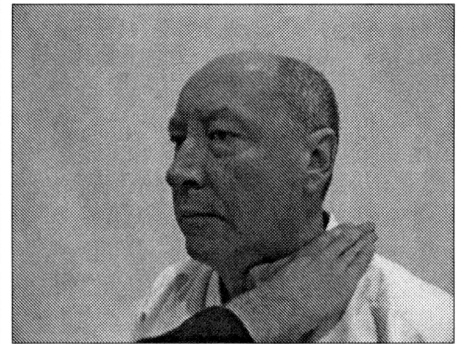
Pic 2.12.8

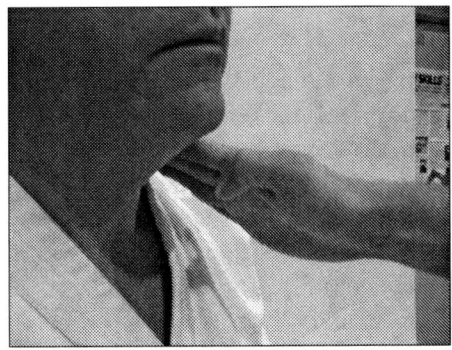
Pic 2.12.9

Pic 2.12.10

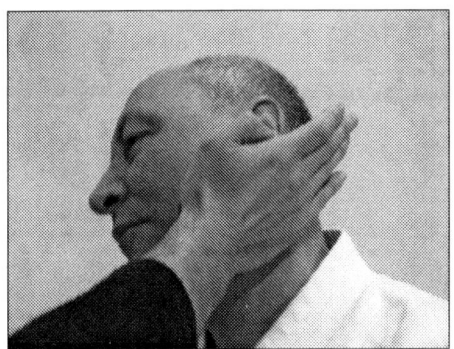
Pic 2.12.11

Effectiveness	Comment
HAOV	One of the most common attacks recorded.
Multiplicity	The techniques can be used in multiple situations.
Predictable Response	This technique makes use of the natural body reaction to a sharp blow to the sternum.
Initiative	The drill begins with a reactive rather than proactive response, but once the initiative is taken it is maintained through a flurry of strikes.

Effectiveness	Comment
Redundancy	This drill assumes the failure of the knife hand strike and immediately flows into a flurried sequence of three strikes to disorientate and drop an opponent. The initial strike could also be followed by a directional change and cross body strike with a left knife hand receiver as per Drill 7. If the attacker begins to drop following the knife hand receiver then the elbow strike (if followed through quickly enough) will catch the face rather than the chest.
Vital Points	Potential strikes to the bicep, LU 7, ST 9, CO 18, SI 16, ST 5, GB 2, GB 1, ear, SP 10, CV 14 and control via CO 10.
Unbalancing	Potential strikes to SP 10 to unbalance from below and CV14 and/or ear to unbalance from above.
Adrenaline Tolerant	Yes. This drill works with a natural flinch reflex. The bicep strike may be lost under severe stress but in that instance the sternum strike should follow naturally or the triple uppercut sequence developed in Drill 4.
Low Maintenance	Yes. Easy to practise solo or paired.
Transferable skills	Uses movements from Drills 5 and 7.

Drill 13

Blue and White face each other in left fences (Pic 2.13.1).

Pic 2.13.1

Pic 2.13.2
(H2.25)

Pic 2.13.3
(H2.25)

White steps in (or simply crosses on the spot) with a right haymaker to Blue's head. A stops this with a left interceptor (Pic 2.13.2) and immediately strikes down and back into White's left forearm while pulling on the attacking limb with his retracting left arm (Pic 2.13.3). Blue's right arm then flicks in circular manner to strike White's right temple (Pic 2.13.4). Blue follows though with a right kick to White's abdomen (Pic 2.13.5) and a left cross (Pic 2.13.6).

Pic 2.13.4
(H2.26)

Pic 2.13.5
(H2.27)

Pic 2.13.6
(H2.28)

Heian Nidan

For the sake of the basic exercise (at this level) White palms aside the left cross with his right arm (alternatively White could lean backwards and to the side to evade the attack so that Blue's following technique acts as a corrective head strike) (Pic 2.13.7). Since Blue's striking arm is relaxed, Blue adapts instantly to the palm by allowing his arm to hinge at the elbow and curve back into an overhand reverse inside receiver strike to White's nose (Pic 2.13.8). Blue follows through with a low left front kick to White's inside leg or groin (Pic 2.13.9), finishing with a right cross (Pic 2.13.10). Blue then steps forward with his right leg into White, striking into his ribs with his left hand while his right fist strikes into his temple with an inside receiver (Pic 2.13.11).

Pic 2.13.7
(H2.28)

Pic 2.13.8
(H2.30)

Pic 2.13.9
(H2.31)

Pic 2.13.10
(H2.32)

Pic 2.13.11
(H2.34)

Effectiveness	Comment
HAOV	One of the most common attacks recorded.
Multiplicity	The techniques can be used in multiple situations.
Predictable Response	Works with the expected body movements following each strike used.
Initiative	Can be proactive or reactive. Once the initiative is taken it is maintained through a flurry of multidirectional strikes.
Redundancy	The drill is set up so that each technique is designed to drop the attacker but has a follow through in the event of failure. A high level of redundancy exists therefore. By training for failure we prepare for success.
Vital Points	Potential strikes to CO 10, ST3, GB 2, GB 1, ear, ST 5, SI 16, CO 18, CO 19, genitalia.
Unbalancing	Potential unbalancing from above from the strike to CO 10 and ear. Potential unbalancing from below through kick to SP 10 or genitalia.
Adrenaline Tolerant	The hand strikes are generally adrenaline tolerant as these techniques should be well rehearsed and make use of transferable skills. Without sufficient practice at close range the kicking techniques may become adrenaline intolerant although their low level works in their favour.
Low Maintenance	Yes, easy to practise solo or paired.
Transferable skills	Uses movements from Drills 5, 6, 7 and 12.

Drill 14

Blue and White face each other in left fences (Pic 2.14.1).

Pic 2.14.1   Pic 2.14.2   Pic 2.14.3
                          (H2.35)   (H2.36)

Blue grabs hold of White's left forearm with his left hand and executes a downsweep to the left, leading White that way (Pic 2.14.2). Blue then pulls his arm 45 degrees to the right and up (possibly with White's hand still attached due to White's natural reflex to pull back) striking into either White's neck or face with a ridge hand (Pic 2.14.3). Without pause Blue immediately steps forward to the right 45 degrees into the side of White, striking into his thigh with his stepping knee (Pic 2.14.4). If White's arm is still forward Blue can upward receiver into White's kidneys, but if White's arm has come back the right hand upward receiver can punch into the side of the neck (Pic 2.14.5). Completing the upward receiver with a ridgehand strike to White's temple, Blue applies pressure with the bony edge of his left thumb and wrist to the right hand side of White's neck while pushing the outside of his right forearm and wrist into the opposite side, strangling White (Pic 2.14.6).

Pic 2.14.4 (H2.37)   Pic 2.14.5 (H2.37)   Pic 2.14.6 (H2.37)

Effectiveness	Comment
HAOV	Not applicable.
Multiplicity	The individual techniques that make up this drill can be used in a multiple of ways. This drill can also be applied following a parry to the inside if the opponent's parrying hand can be grabbed.
Predictable Response	This drill anticipates White's intention to pull back his hand.
Initiative	This is a proactive drill that takes the initiative and then keeps it with multiple strikes and a strangle.
Redundancy	Strangulation technique in case body and head strikes have not dropped opponent. All the techniques used have high levels of redundancy.
Vital Points	Potential strikes to GB 32, LR 13, BL 49, BL 50, BL 51, ST 3, GB 1, GB 2, Mind point.

Effectiveness	Comment
Unbalancing	Potential unbalancing through stepping strike to GB 32.
Adrenaline Tolerant	Yes, requires very little skill to execute and makes use of well-rehearsed skills. The greatest bar to this technique is not adrenaline but the mental attitude of the practitioner, without sufficient drilling many may find it impossible to begin the physical part of the fight themselves.
Low Maintenance	Strangulation techniques may require regular practice – it is important for safety reasons that students learn to count as soon as they apply the technique.
Transferable skills	Uses a directional change similar to Drill 7.

Drill 15

Blue and White face each other in left fences (Pic 2.15.1).

White steps in (or simply crosses on the spot) with a right haymaker to Blue's head. Blue stops this with a left interceptor (Pic 2.15.2) and immediately strikes down and back into White's left forearm with his right hand while pulling on the attacking limb with his retracting left arm (Pic 2.15.3). Blue's right arm then flicks in circular manner to strike White's right temple.

Pic 2.15.1

Pic 2.15.2
(H2.25)

Pic 2.15.3
(H2.25)

White intercepts this by moving his free left hand across to the right hand side of his face, thus with his right arm already extended forming the preparation movement for a down sweep, White now moves into Drill 9 (Pic 2.15.4).

Pic 2.15.4
(H2.26 & White-H1.2)

White strikes out into Blue's left temple with his left fist while pulling back on Blue's left arm with his right Pic (2.15.5). White then grabs the back of Blue's neck with his left hand and strikes with his right knee into Blue's thigh or groin (Pic 2.15.6). White then steps down and punches Blue at any available target with his right fist (Pic 2.15.7).

 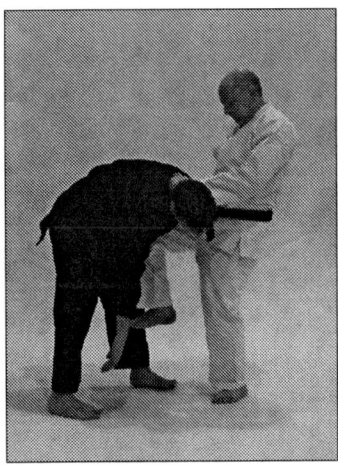 

Pic 2.15.5   Pic 2.15.6   Pic 2.15.7
(White H1.3)   (White H1.4)   (White H1.4)

Once taught there should be no prior agreement between Blue and White as to whether 13 or 15 is to be followed – the fastest mover determines this.

Effectiveness	**Comment**
HAOV	One of the most common attacks recorded.
Multiplicity	The techniques can be used in multiple situations.
Predictable Response	Works with the expected body movements following each strike used.
Initiative	Can be proactive or reactive. This drill trains methods of recovering lost initiative in mid fight scenarios.
Redundancy	If B hesitates to follow through from the parry then the pre-existing drill of the kick should take the initiative back to A.
Vital Points	Potential strikes to CO 10, ST3, GB 2, GB 1, ear, ST 5, SI 16, CO 18, CO 19.
Unbalancing	Potential unbalancing from above from the strike to CO 10 and ear.
Adrenaline Tolerant	The hand strikes are generally adrenaline tolerant as these techniques should be well rehearsed and make use of transferable skills. Without sufficient practice at close range the kicking techniques may become adrenaline intolerant although their low level works in their favour.
Low Maintenance	Yes, easy to practise solo or paired.
Transferable skills	Uses movements from Drills 9 and 13.

Advanced points

The bicep attack should aim to strike at LU 4.

The knee strike should attack the thigh at GB 32 while the follow through kick should aim for BL 57.

Once students have mastered the rigid forms of the drills as set out above on both sides, they should then begin to experiment with intercepting each other's counter-attacks using the techniques taught thus far.

Occasionally, practicing the techniques slowly paired up at triple the distance (so no contact is actually made) can often give students greater opportunity to analyse whether they are making best use of their stances and hips. It also leads to a greater ability to visualise an opponent – an essential part of solo training.

Heian Sandan

The kata movements

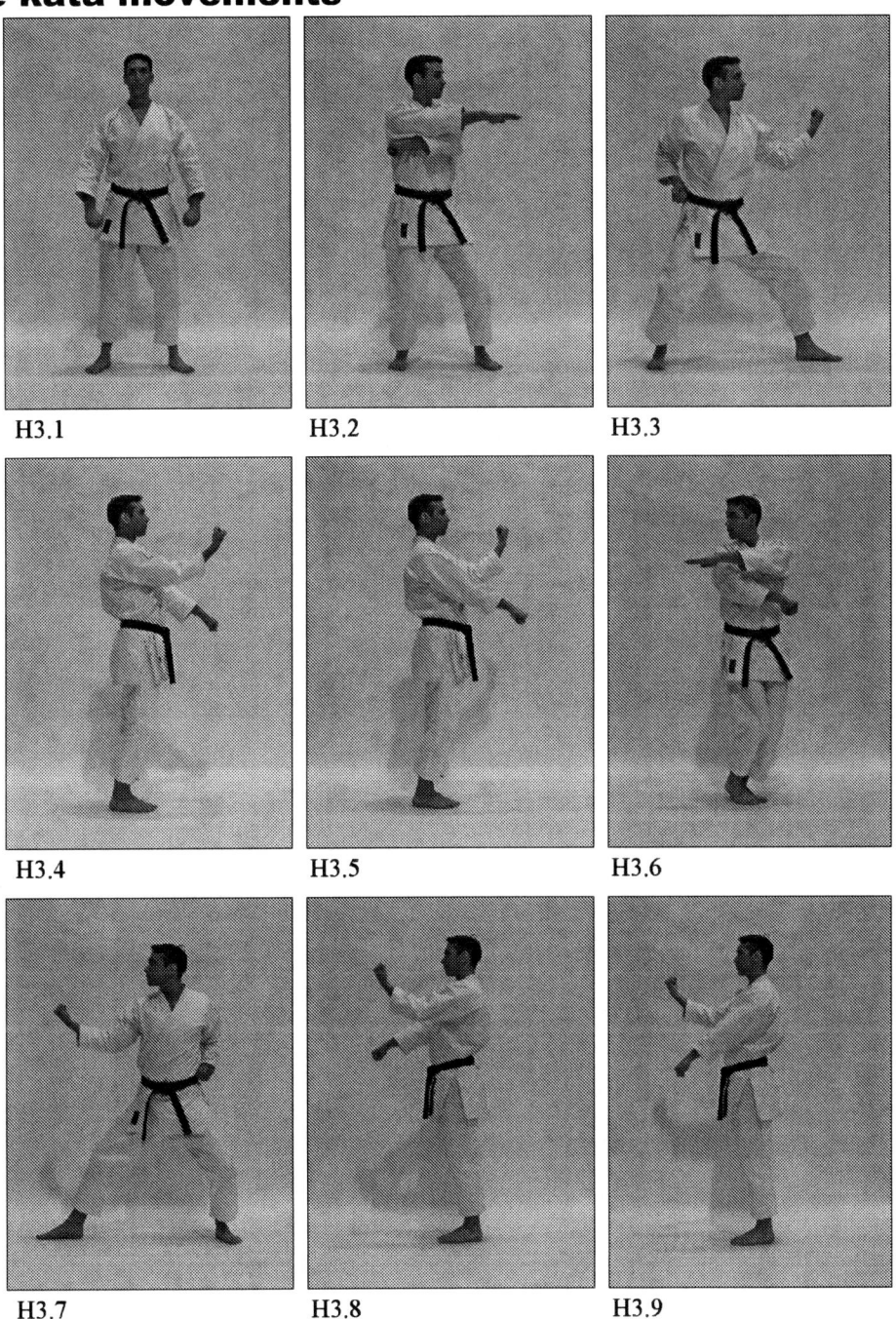

Heian Sandan

H3.10 H3.11 H3.12

H3.13 H3.14 H3.15

H3.16 H3.17 H3.18

Heian Sandan

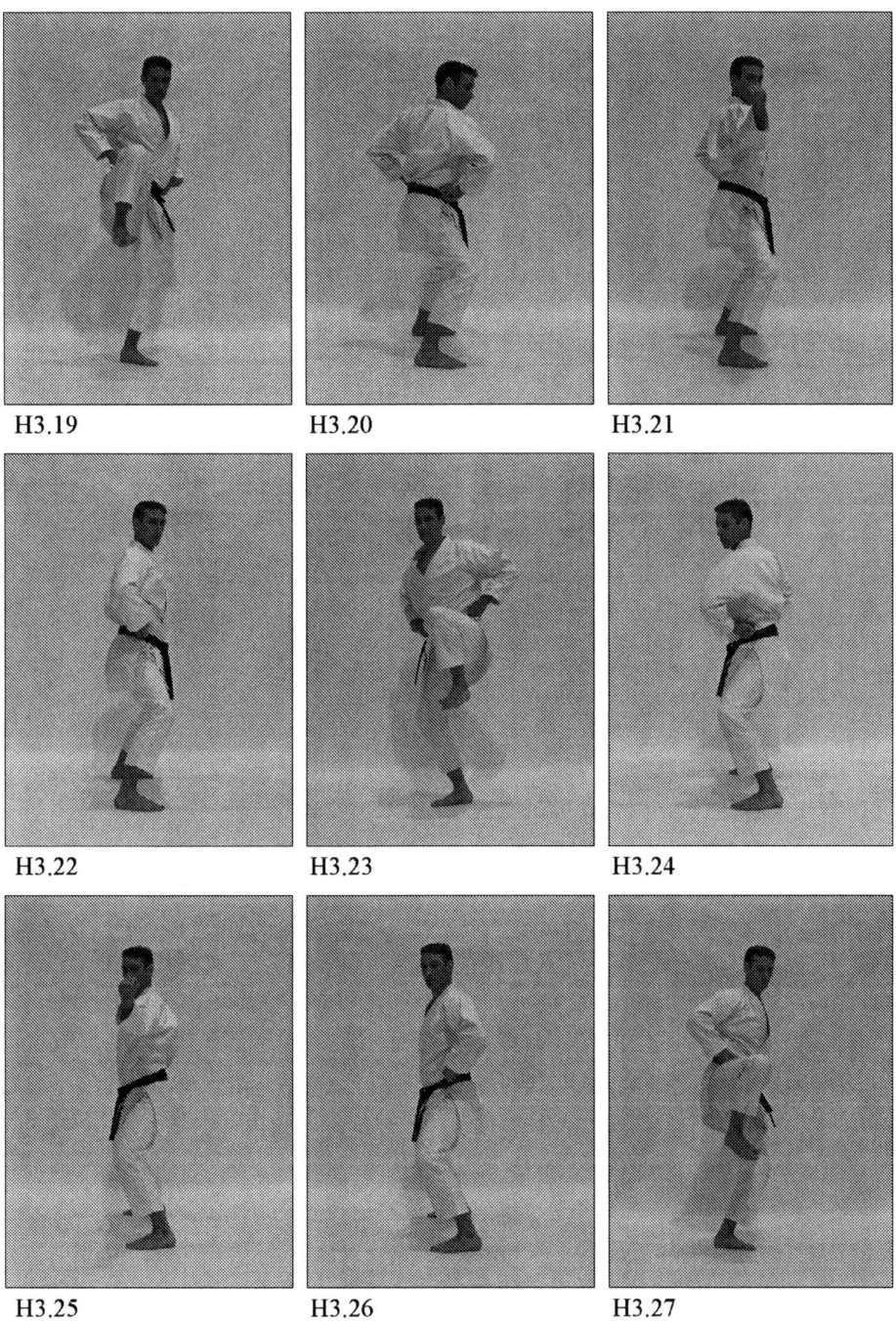

H3.19   H3.20   H3.21

H3.22   H3.23   H3.24

H3.25   H3.26   H3.27

Heian Sandan

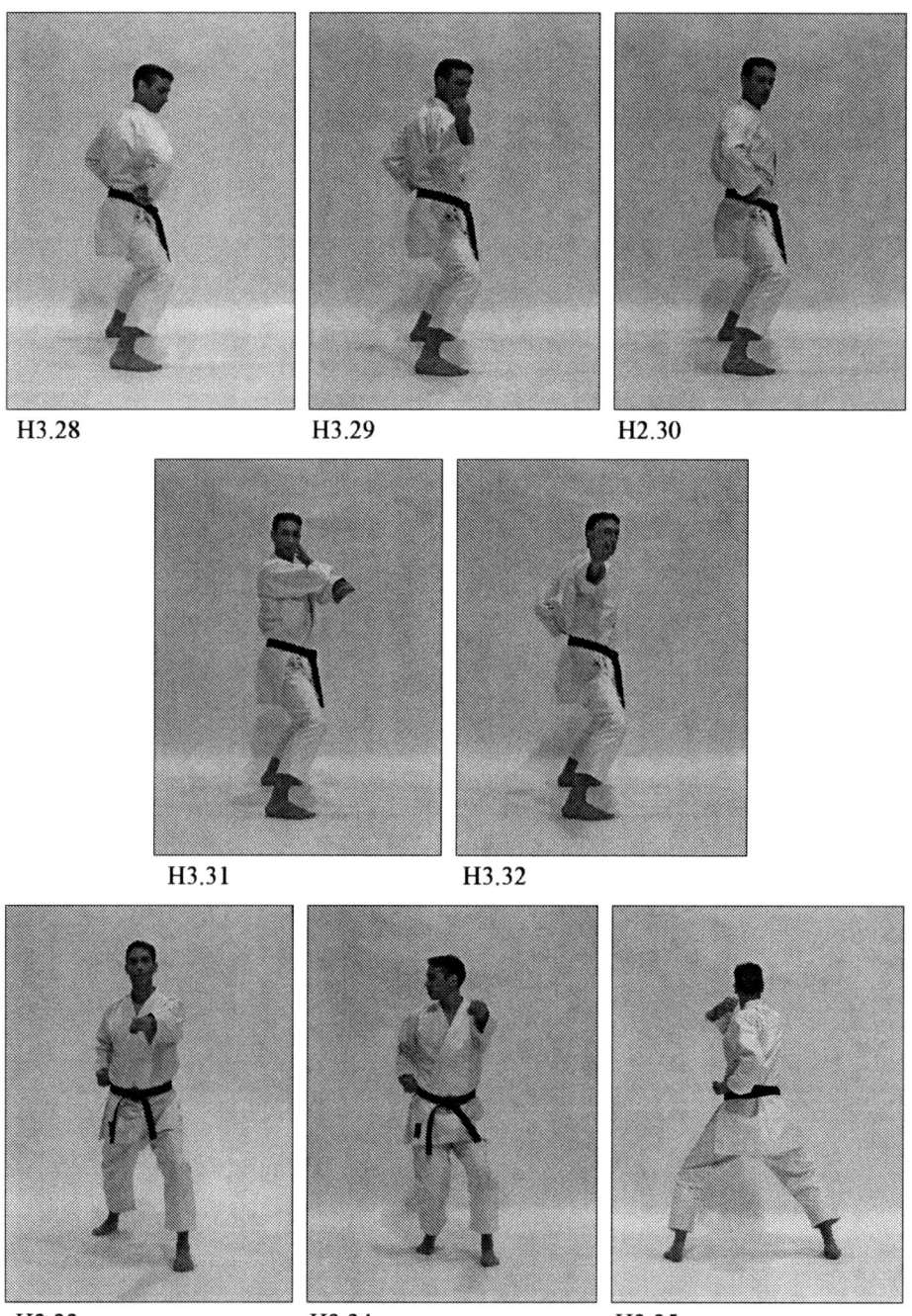

H3.28　　　　　H3.29　　　　　H2.30

H3.31　　　　　H3.32

H3.33　　　　　H3.34　　　　　H3.35

H3.36 H3.37 H3.38

Training rationale

Please note that all drills should be practiced on both sides, however students should give prominence to defending from their habitual fence. To ensure a level of realism and technique flow, when struck practitioners are asked to simulate a 50-70% successful blow, thus folding over in response to punches or head strikes but not dropping completely as per a knockout. This allows students to train to follow through naturally from one technique into another with a more realistic body position that is not provided by a purely rigid training partner. In many instances these people make a remarkable recovery midway through the drills, but this serves to keep both practitioners on their toes. The simulation of the body's reaction to actual strikes also teaches students about how the body is likely to move, serves as mental preparation for real events and improves visualisation skills.

The Sandan drills are the core of the Heian Flow System, teaching students how to make a natural transition between ballistic and grappling techniques.

The purpose of the Heian Sandan drills is as follows:

- To introduce pre-emptive striking with multiple redundancy patterns in a free flowing situation.
- To introduce students to moving with a partner to absorb energy and accustom them to responding to unbalancing techniques such as shoves.
- To work the concept of striking available targets such as the limbs to open further targets.
- To teach students to use circular strikes and double arm strikes to exploit the weaknesses of tunnel vision.
- To accustom students to non-linear methods of movement.
- To introduce new locking and control techniques.
- To introduce techniques designed to escape dangerous mid and end game positions.
- To increase the element of unpredictability in paired training.

Changes to the kata movement in the Heian Flow System

Sequences of movements are either initiated from a fence or a middle or end game fighting position instead of/in addition to the preceding movement in the Kata.

Heian Sandan drills

Drill 16

Cross body push:

White pushes Blue's right shoulder with his right hand (Pic 3.16.1). Blue moves his right shoulder back with the energy of the push (twisting his waist and shifting his weight to allow the force to push through him without moving his feet) and simultaneously raises his left fist in a vertical inside receiver striking across White's extended arm and into his nose with the back of his knuckles (increased forward momentum by White will result in Blues forearm or elbow making contact) (Pic 3.16.2). Blue immediately follows through by sweeping White's right arm down with a left arm downsweep as he simultaneously strikes into White's right temple with a right inside receiver (alternatively this arm can use a similar motion to uppercut into B's chin – in either case the full force of a return body twist - like a pendulum swinging back – should be applied) (Pic 3.16.3). If Blue has not fully dropped White or White is merely bent over, Blue can then lift White's right arm upwards with his left arm while striking down with his right fist in a down sweep motion into either White's temple or abdomen (depending upon White's position) (Pic 3.16.4).

Pic 3.16.1

Pic 3.16.2
(H3.3)

Pic 3.16.3   Pic 3.16.4
(H3.4)   (H3.5)

This sequence can also be applied if a cross body push is applied to the rear shoulder.

Effectiveness	**Comment**
HAOV	The push is the most commonly recorded act of male on male violence. It is often followed directly by a punch.
Multiplicity	The techniques in this drill can be used against both a cross or opposite push (see Drill 17). They may also be used against a two handed push and can even be employed in a mid-game situation whenever the lead arm is inside or outside the attacker's arm in the manner shown here.
Predictable Response	This drill anticipates a probable punching follow up by the non-pushing arm and thus, although it moves into the likely arc of such a technique, uses a strike that can act as a block for such an attack.

Effectiveness	Comment
Initiative	This drill is reactive rather than proactive but responds quickly to the stimulus to take and keep the initiative with multiple strikes. The drill can also be used to regain the initiative in a mid game situation.
Redundancy	This drill consists of multiple striking techniques so that if one fails the practitioner is automatically moving into an appropriate follow up. The right inside receiver strike to the head may also double as a block if the attacker has time to follow the push with a punch.
Vital Points	Potential strikes to the golgi tendon, temple, ST 3, mind point, GB 2, GB 1, LU 7, LR 13, LR 14, ST 5, ear. The range of targets depends upon whether the initial right hand strike hits the arm or the head and the subsequent position of both the body and the head.
Unbalancing	The swift movement of the body following the push and the simultaneous strike to the extended arm may cause the attacker to be unbalanced depending upon how far their weight is committed into the push. The potential strike to the ear will, if achieved, cause the attacker to drop.
Adrenaline Tolerant	Moderate. This Drill often causes an adverse adrenaline reaction in students to begin with due to the shock of the push. This is precisely why it is so important to drill against pushes (and why many of the Heian Shodan Drills end with pushes). With regular drilling students become comfortable with being pushed and it no longer causes such an adrenaline reaction so adverse as to incapacitate the practitioner.
Low Maintenance	This technique is low maintenance.

Effectiveness	Comment
Transferable skills	Many of the arm movements used in this drill occur in other drills such as Drill 17, Drill 33 and 34.

Drill 17

Opposite push:

White pushes Blue's right shoulder with his left hand (Pic 3.17.1). Blue moves his right shoulder and twists to absorb the energy of the push and simultaneously with his left fist backfist strikes White's nose or temple (Pic 3.17.2). Blue immediately follows through by pivoting back through his original position in a reverse counter-clockwise twist as his left arm curves over White's extended left before moving in a down sweep, pivoting White's body round in a clockwise motion, moving his right arm at the same time as his left to strike White's left temple (Pic 3.17.3). If Blue has not fully dropped White or White is merely bent over, Blue can grip White's left wrist and pull it upwards as his right elbow and forearm apply downwards pressure to the back of White's left shoulder in a down sweep before his right fist connects with White's left temple (Pic 3.17.4).

Pic 3.17.1

Pic 3.17.2
(H3.3)

Pic 3.17.3 (H3.4)   Pic 3.17.4 (H3.5)

This sequence can be applied if an opposite push is applied to the rear shoulder.

Effectiveness	**Comment**
HAOV	The push is the most commonly recorded act of male on male violence. It is often followed directly by a punch.
Multiplicity	The techniques in this drill can be used against both a cross or opposite push (see Drill 16). They may also be used against a two handed push and can even be employed in a mid-game situation whenever the lead arm is inside or outside the attacker's arm in the manner shown here.
Predictable Response	This drill anticipates a probable punching follow up by the non-pushing arm and thus moves outside the likely arc of such a technique with an immediate head strike. The final strike of this drill anticipates the likely position of the attacker's body following a semi successful preceding strike.

Effectiveness	Comment
Initiative	In the context here the drill is reactive rather than proactive, moving swiftly to take the initiative with a flurry of strikes and an arm control. The techniques of this drill can be used proactively however.
Redundancy	This drill consists of multiple strikes so that if one fails the practitioner is trained to follow up without pause. The arm control position also enables the practitioner to flow immediately into the arm bar in Drill 20.
Vital Points	Potential strikes to CO 19, CO 10, LU 5, ST 3, mind point, GB 2, GB 1, LU 7, ST 5, ear.
Unbalancing	This drill unbalances from above by pressure applied to the shoulder blade from behind with simultaneous manipulation of the arm. An on target strike to the ear will most likely cause the attacker to drop.
Adrenaline Tolerant	Moderate. This drill often causes an adverse adrenaline reaction in students to begin with due to the shock of the push. This is precisely why it is so important to drill against pushes (and why many of the Heian Shodan drills end with pushes). With regular drilling students become comfortable with being pushed and it no longer causes such an adrenaline reaction so adverse as to incapacitate the practitioner.
Low Maintenance	This drill is low maintenance.
Transferable skills	Many of the arm movements used in this drill occur in other drills such as Drills 16, 33 and 24.

Drill 18

White grabs Blue's right lapel with his left hand (Pic 3.18.1).

Blue attacks White pre-emptively, stepping forward with his left leg (keeping his weight on his right for stability) and bringing his left arm across his body to cover any head or arm attacks by White before turning it in a reverse direction to strike White's left temple with an inside receiver. At the same time Blue drives his right fist into White's ribs in an uppercut (Pic 3.18.2).

Pic 3.18.1   Pic 3.18.2
                     (H3.11)

This should drop White, but for the purposes of the drill Blue is trained to follow though anticipating failure by flowing from one strike automatically into the next.

Blue follows through by dropping his left fist to strike the top of White's left bicep (Pic 3.18.3) before striking White's sternum with a left elbow strike (Pic 3.18.4), knocking White back. Blue steps forward to strike either White's neck or face with a right spear hand strike (Pic 3.18.5).

Pic 3.18.3 (H3.12)   Pic 3.18.4 (H3.12)   Pic 3.18.5 (H3.13)

Effectiveness	Comment
HAOV	A one handed front clothing grab followed by a punch to the head is one of the most commonly recorded attacks.
Multiplicity	This drill can be used pre-emptively without any grab either to initiate a fight or from a free position in a mid-game situation. It can also be used outside (as opposed to inside) the attacker's arms, albeit less effectively.
Predictable Response	This drill anticipates the likely body movement following each strike and follows through with a technique appropriate to the target position.

Effectiveness	Comment
Initiative	This drill scores highly since although it responds to a grab, it is proactive in not waiting for any subsequent percussive technique. Once the drill begins it maintains the initiative with a flurry of strikes to multiple targets at different levels to confuse, disorientate and disable the attacker. The techniques of this drill may also be used proactively without waiting for any lapel grab.
Redundancy	The opening technique consists of two strikes so that in the unlikely event that one is deflected, the other is likely to hit its own target and thus buy the time to move through with the next strike. The multiple strikes drilled ensure that if anything fails at one level there is an automatic follow up. Drills 28 and 35 train redundancy scenarios for a severe failure of the sternum strike in this drill and Drills 19, 20, 21, 22, 23 and 32 for the parrying of the spear hand strike (and Drill 11 can also be used in this event). The left inside receiver has the potential to smother any percussive technique in the event of the action being initiated too late and the direction of the step with its attacks mean that such a punch will not make contact due to the counter force applied to the attacker's body.
Vital Points	Potential strikes to LU 7, LR 13, LR 14, SP 10, GB 1, GB 2, mind point, ST3, SI 17, CO 18, LU 5, Bicep, CV 14, ST 9, ST 5, ear.
Unbalancing	This drill unbalances from below with a stepping strike to SP 10 and from above with a strike to CV 14 and a circular strike to the ear.

Effectiveness	Comment
Adrenaline Tolerant	Yes. The techniques used are simple and easy to execute. There is a possibility that under severe stress the bicep strike may be skipped in the hurry to move to the sternum strike, but those strikes are only redundancies in the event of the initial strike failing. To execute this drill it is important that the practitioner recognise that a grab is a physical attack that requires an immediate response.
Low Maintenance	The techniques of this drill are so common throughout the drills of the Heian Flow System that they are very low maintenance.
Transferable skills	This drill utilises techniques (and entire sequences) already developed in Drills 12, 13, 16 and 17. Its techniques are used in many subsequent drills.

Drill 19

As Drill 18 but with White moving in different ways to challenge Blue.

Pic 3.19.1 (H3.13)   Pic 3.19.2 (H3.14)   Pic 3.19.3 (H3.14)

As Blue steps in with the right spear hand strike White avoids the strike by palming it to the right with his left hand (Pic 3.19.1). Blue immediately drops his diverted hand into either a ridge hand strike into the inside of White's leg near the knee (SP 10) (Pic 3.19.2) or into an upward slap into White's genitals (Pic 3.19.3).

Twisting in a counter clockwise fashion round the back of White, Blue follows this with a left rear elbow strike to White's head (Pic 3.19.4), before grabbing White's head with his left hand (Pic 3.19.5) and, stepping forward, punching the back of his neck with his right fist (Pic 3.19.6) before wrapping his right arm round White's neck in a headlock (Pic 3.19.7). The strike to the back of the neck is usually done to GB20, any strike to the spine in this way could result in paralysis or death so care must be taken in drilling.

Pic 3.19.4 (H3.15)   Pic 3.19.5 (H3.15)   Pic 3.19.6 (H3.16)

White immediately pushes his head back to prevent any pressure being applied to the back of his neck while pulling on Blue's right arm with his own. White then slams his left elbow into Blue's thigh at GB32 (Pic 3.19.8) before arching it over and upwards to strike into Blue's genitals (Pic 3.19.9) before bringing it back towards him to strike into the inside of Blue's leg with his fist at SP 10 (Pic 3.19.10).

Pic 3.19.7
(H3.17)

Pic 3.19.8
(White H3.20)

Pic 3.19.9
(White H3.21)

Pic 3.19.10
(White H3.22)

Pic 3.19.11
(White H3.22)

Pic 3.19.12
(White H3.23)

White then pushes back through the loosened hold, transferring his grip of Blue's right wrist from his right hand to his left (Pic 3.19.11). White then steps forward and down into Blue with his right leg striking Blue's face with either a crescent kick or a knee strike (Pic 3.19.12). White then keeps Blue's wrist locked tight at his left hip with his left hand and applies a straight arm bar with his right forearm (Pic 3.19.13). White then backfists the back of Blue's neck with his right fist (Pic 3.19.14) and reapplies the straight arm bar (Pic 3.19.15).

Pic 3.19.13 (White H3.24)   Pic 3.19.14 (White H3.25)   Pic 3.19.15 (White H3.26)

Effectiveness	Comment
HAOV	A one handed front clothing grab followed by a punch to the head is one of the most commonly recorded attacks. The grappling style headlock, although less prevalent, is another commonly recorded form of attack and unlike the clothing grab is more likely to occur in the mid-game or end-game stage of a fight.
Multiplicity	The initial movement of this drill relies on a particular position and/or technique failure and thus has limited multiplicity. The subsequent sequence of techniques (attacking from behind and breaking out from a chancery headlock can be used in many mid game scenarios or potential end game scenarios.
Predictable Response	This drill anticipates the natural flinch reflex for a straight lunge to the face. The end stage of this drill anticipates the physical reaction to strikes to the leg and groin.

Effectiveness	Comment
Initiative	This drill regains the initiative following a failed strike by a change of direction and a flurry of strikes at different levels to disorientate and disable.
Redundancy	This drill is the redundancy for the failure of the finishing strike in Drill 18 and any situation where the forward hand has been palmed to the inside from its outside. The drill consists of multiple strikes so that if one fails there is an automatic counter. Redundancies for the failure of the techniques of this drill are provided by Drills 20, 21 and 22.
Vital Points	Potential strikes to ST 3, ST 5, SP 10, GB 1, GB 2, mind point, GB 20, BL 49, BL50, BL 51, ear, genitalia, GB 32, control at the golgi tendon.
Unbalancing	Potential unbalancing through strikes to SP 10, genitalia, GB 32, ear and control of the arm through a straight arm bar.
Adrenaline Tolerant	Yes
Low Maintenance	This drill does not require any specialised skills and is low maintenance.
Transferable skills	The techniques in this drill are also used in Drills 12, 18, 20, 21 and 22.

Drill 20

As Blue steps in with the right spear hand strike White avoids the strike by palming it to the right with his left hand (Pic 3.20.1). Blue immediately drops his diverted hand attempting either a ridge hand strike into the inside of White's leg near the knee (SP 10) or into an upward slap into White's genitals, but White steps back to avoid this (Pic 3.20.2). Twisting in a counter clockwise fashion, Blue attempts to follow this with a left rear elbow strike to White's

Heian Sandan

head but sensing White's movement Blue extends his elbow strike into a hammer fist but this is stopped by White's right arm (Pic 3.20.3).

Pic 3.20.1
(H3.13)

Pic 3.20.2
(H3.14)

Pic 3.20.3
(H3.15)

Blue promptly attempts to elbow strike to White's face with his left elbow, causing White to push against his wrist (and possibly even grab) with his left hand in defence (Pic 3.20.4). If White is not fast enough Blue should make the elbow strike. From this or the forced deflection of the strike there are two variations:

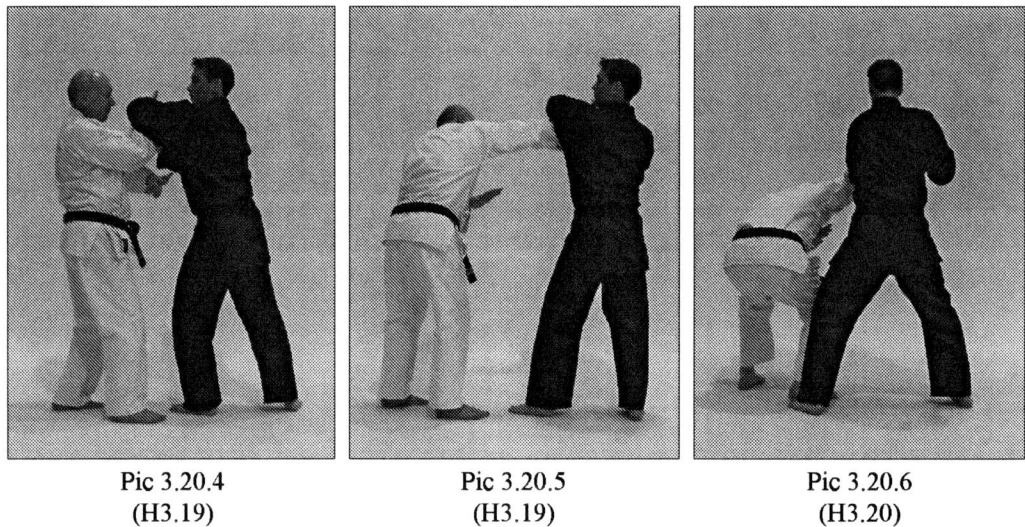

Pic 3.20.4
(H3.19)

Pic 3.20.5
(H3.19)

Pic 3.20.6
(H3.20)

Variation 1. If White's arm is straight or almost straight, Blue rolls White's right hand clockwise so that it is palm upwards and draws it to the centre of his chest (ensuring that it is straight – this is easy if White is trying to push away an elbow strike) so that his right hand can take control of the back of the hand and wrist (Pic 3.20.5). Blue then steps into and behind White (this could be led by a crescent kick to the back of White's leg), sinking his weight and applying force to the back of White's extended arm to create a straight arm bar (Pic 3.20.6).

Maintaining control of White's arm with his right hand Blue backfists down onto the back of White's neck with his right fist (Pic 3.20.7) before retracting it to apply further pressure to the straight arm bar (Pic 3.20.8). It is important to note that the depth of the stance employed will affect the pressure level of the lock and that this technique could become a break if executed with full power. The high stance shown here reflects the mobility of White's shoulder joint, consequently this technique should be executed slowly initially in training to avoid unnecessary injuries.

Pic 3.20.7
(H3.21)

Pic 3.20.8
(H3.22)

Pic 3.20.9
(H3.19)

Variation 2. If White's arm is bent, Blue rolls White's right hand clockwise so that it is palm upwards and draws it to the centre of his chest so that his right hand can take control of the back of the hand. From this position Blue rolls his left forearm over the top of White's right forearm and then back towards him, creating an effective S bend lock (Pic 3.20.9 and 3.20.10). Blue follows this with a circular knee strike to White with his right leg (Pic 3.20.11). Blue can finish with a downward right roundhouse elbow to White's head (Pic 3.20.12).

Pic 3.20.10 (H3.20)   Pic 3.20.11 (H3.23)   Pic 3.20.12 (H3.24)

Effectiveness	Comment
HAOV	A one handed front clothing grab followed by a punch to the head is one of the most commonly recorded attacks.
Multiplicity	The initial movement of this drill relies on a particular position and/or technique failure and thus has limited multiplicity. The subsequent sequence of techniques (both the straight arm bar and the s bend lock) can be used in multiple situations.
Predictable Response	This drill anticipates the natural flinch reflex for a straight lunge to the face. The locking techniques anticipate the natural flinch response to grab a hand near the face. The follow up to both the straight arm bar and the S bend lock anticipate the likely position of the recipient.

Effectiveness	Comment
Initiative	This drill regains the initiative following a failed strike by a change of direction and an attempted strike. With the failure of the second strike the initiative is regained by moving from percussive to grappling techniques. Both Variation 1 and variation 2 can be applied as pre-emptive responses to grabs to the arm, chest or shoulder.
Redundancy	This drill is the redundancy for the failure of the finishing strike in Drill 18 and any situation where a hand has been palmed to the inside. The two variations act as redundancies for each other and Drills 21, 23 and 36 act as a redundancy for failure to apply any lock at all.
Vital Points	Potential strikes to SP 10, GB 20, BL1, BL 2, Mind point, ST 3, ST 5, ear.
Unbalancing	Potential to unbalance from below with the hand strike to SP 10 and potential to unbalance from above with both the straight arm bar and the S bend lock and the strike to the ear.
Adrenaline Tolerant	Moderate. The locking techniques at the end will probably be ineffectual under the influence of adrenaline if they have not been rigorously drilled.
Low Maintenance	Although the movements for the controls can be rehearsed solo only paired practice will generate the necessary skill level.
Transferable skills	This drill rehearses skills used in preceding and subsequent drills.

Drill 21

As Blue steps in with the right spear hand strike White avoids the strike by palming it to the right with his left hand (Pic 3.21.1). Blue immediately drops his diverted hand, attempting either a ridge hand strike into the inside of White's leg near the knee (SP 10) or into an upward slap into White's genitals, but White steps back to avoid this (Pic 3.21.2). Twisting in a counter clockwise fashion, Blue attempts to follow this with a left rear elbow strike to White's head but sensing White's movement Blue extends his elbow strike into a hammer fist but this is stopped by White's right arm (Pic 3.21.3).

Blue promptly steps in with a right uppercut into White's ribs, pulling him by grabbing White's right arm with his left hand (Pic 3.21.4). Blue follows the punch by turning counter-clockwise into White, drawing White's right arm tight across his (Blue's) with White's right hand at Blue's left hip and Blue's deltoid/upper triceps in White's armpit (note White's weight is not put across Blue's collar bone) and throwing him with a backward thrust of his hips (Pic 3.21.5). Blue maintains control and distance with White by keeping hold of White's wrist (Pic 3.21.6). Blue stamps onto White's sternum with his heel (Pic 3.21.7).

Pic 3.21.1   Pic 3.21.2   Pic 3.21.3
(H3.13)   (H3.14)   (H3.15)

Pic 3.21.4
(H3.16)

Pic 3.21.5
(H3.17)

Pic 3.21.6
(H3.19)

Pic 3.21.7
(H3.20)

Effectiveness	**Comment**
HAOV	A one handed front clothing grab followed by a punch to the head is one of the most commonly recorded attacks.
Multiplicity	The throw in this drill can be used in multiple situations.

Effectiveness	Comment
Predictable Response	This drill anticipates the natural flinch reflex for a straight lunge to the face.
Initiative	This drill seeks to regain the initiative following a failed strike and on the failure of this attempts to do so once more with a (hopefully unanticipated) change of tactics.
Redundancy	If the step work places the practitioner too far to the outside to contemplate the throw then the drill can be substituted by Drill 20. If the practitioner does not feel confident with the throw (perhaps due to the size of the assailant) Drill 13 provides a ballistic redundancy. Drill 21 itself is a redundancy for Drills 18, 19 and 20. The throw at the end of this drill is a redundant technique for an ineffective preceding punch to the abdomen or chest.
Vital Points	Potential strikes to SP 10, LR 13, LR14 and CV14.
Unbalancing	Potential unbalancing through hand strike to SP 10 and through throwing technique.
Adrenaline Tolerant	Yes.
Low Maintenance	Requires regular practice of throwing technique to maintain competency.
Transferable skills	Utilises skills used in preceding and subsequent drills.

Drill 22

As Blue steps in with the right spear hand strike White avoids the strike by palming it to the right with his left hand (Pic 3.22.1). Blue immediately drops his diverted hand to attempt either a ridge hand strike into the inside of White's leg near the knee (SP 10) or into an upward slap into White's genitals but is blocked by White maintaining contact with his arm and stepping forward (Pic 3.22.2). White meanwhile reaches his right arm up to wrap around Blue's neck as

Blue continues to pivot (Pic 3.22.3). White then tightens his grip to put Blue in a headlock (Pic 3.22.4).

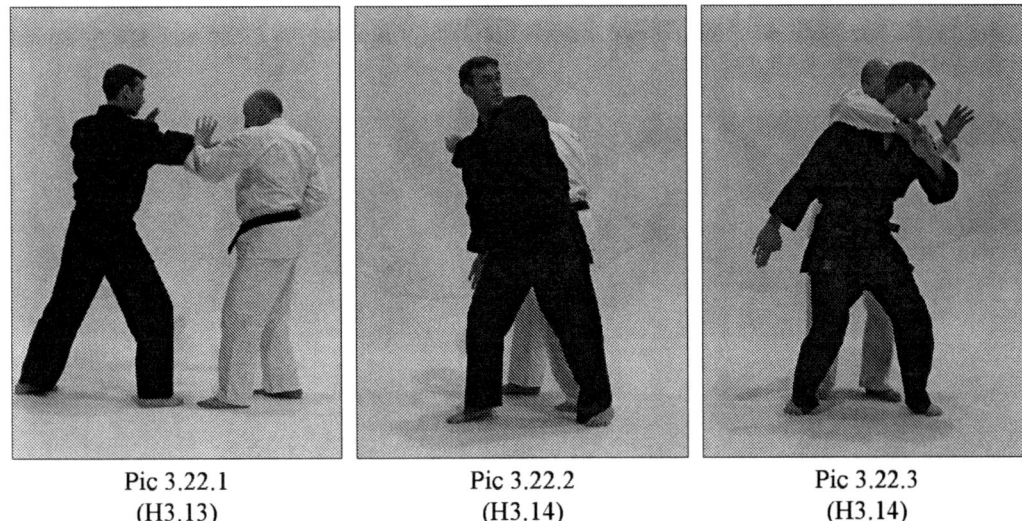

Pic 3.22.1
(H3.13)

Pic 3.22.2
(H3.14)

Pic 3.22.3
(H3.14)

Pic 3.22.4
(H3.24)

Pic 3.22.5
(H3.25)

Pic 3.22.6
(H3.26)

Blue immediately pushes his head back to prevent any pressure being applied to the back of his neck while pulling on White's right arm with his own. Blue then slams his left elbow into White's thigh at GB32 (Pic 3.22.5) before arching it over and upwards to strike into White's genitals (Pic 3.22.6) before bringing it back towards him to strike into the inside of White's leg with his fist at SP 10 (Pic 3.22.7). Blue then pushes back through the loosened hold, transferring his grip of White's right wrist from his right hand to his left (Pic 3.22.8). Blue then steps forward and down into White with his right leg striking White's face with either a crescent kick or a knee strike (Pic 3.22.9). Blue then keeps White's wrist locked tight at his left hip with his left hand and applies a straight arm bar with his right forearm (Pic 3.22.10). Blue then backfists the back of White's neck with his right fist (Pic 3.22.11) and reapplies the straight arm bar (Pic 3.22.12).

Pic 3.22.7
(H3.26)

Pic 3.22.8
(H3.26)

Pic 3.22.9
(H3.27)

Pic 3.22.10
(H3.28)

Pic 3.22.11
(H3.29)

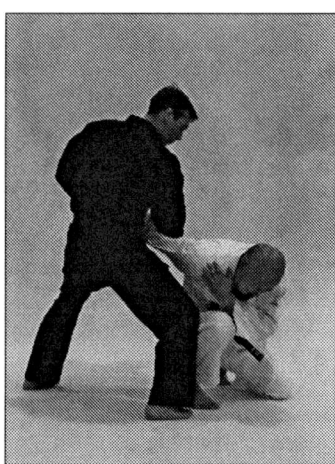
Pic 3.22.12
(H3.30)

Effectiveness	Comment
HAOV	A one handed front clothing grab followed by a punch to the head is one of the most commonly recorded attacks. The grappling style headlock, although less prevalent, is another commonly recorded form of attack and unlike the clothing grab is more likely to occur in the mid-game or end-game stage of a fight.
Multiplicity	The initial movement of this drill relies on a particular position and/or technique failure and thus has limited multiplicity. The subsequent sequence of techniques (attacking from behind and breaking out from a chancery headlock can be used in many mid game scenarios or potential end game scenarios.
Predictable Response	This drill anticipates the natural flinch reflex for a straight lunge to the face. The end stage of this drill anticipates the physical reaction to strikes to the leg and groin.
Initiative	This drill trains practitioners to regain the initiative from two mid-game situations; firstly a failed strike to the head and secondly a grappling style head lock.
Redundancy	This drill anticipates a more proactive opponent who manages to regain the initiative following the defender's strikes. It is thus a redundancy for Drills 18, 19, 20 and 21.
Vital Points	Potential strikes to SP 10, GB 32, genitalia, GB 20, ear, ST3, GB 1, GB 2, ST 5.
Unbalancing	Potential unbalancing from below via strikes to SP 10, genitalia and GB 32. Potential unbalancing from above via crescent kick to the ear.

Effectiveness	Comment
Adrenaline Tolerant	Yes. The technique to break out of the head lock works with natural instincts such as gripping the primary locking arm to ease the choke/strangle and hitting with the other arm.
Low Maintenance	This drill does not require any fine motor skills and is low maintenance.
Transferable skills	Utilises skills used in preceding drills.

Drill 23

As Blue steps in with the right spear hand strike White avoids the strike by palming it to the right with his right hand (Pic 3.23.1).

Pic 3.23.1
(H3.13)

Blue immediately steps in with his left leg and strikes over the top of White's right arm with his left elbow while bringing his right hand back to control White's right wrist.

Variation 1: First and foremost this is an elbow strike to White's head (Pic 3.23.2).

Pic 3.23.2
(H3.24)

Variation 2: White manages to lean back to avoid the short range of the elbow strike (Pic 3.23.3), but Blue rolls his left fist round to the left in an inside receiver to connect with White's left temple (Pic 3.23.4).

Pic 3.23.3   Pic 3.23.4
(H3.24)   (H3.25)

Variation 3: White manages to lean back to avoid the short range of the elbow strike (Pic 3.23.5), but Blue rolls left elbow over White's right arm, while trapping White's right wrist roughly against his chest with his left hand, thus forcing White to the ground in a high S bend lock (Pic 3.23.6). Blue then follows through with a roundhouse knee strike to White's face (Pic 3.23.7) and a downward elbow strike (Pic 3.23.8).

Pic 3.23.5
(H3.24)

Pic 3.23.6
(H3.24)

Pic 3.23.7
(H3.27)

Pic 3.23.8
(H3.28)

Effectiveness	Comment
HAOV	A one handed front clothing grab followed by a punch to the head is one of the most commonly recorded attacks.
Multiplicity	The techniques used in this drill can be employed in multiple situations.

Effectiveness	Comment
Predictable Response	This drill anticipates the natural flinch reflex for a straight lunge to the face.
Initiative	This drill teaches practitioners how to apply previously used opening-game drills in a mid game situation to regain the initiative following a failed strike.
Redundancy	This drill is a redundancy for Drills 15, 16, 17, 18 and 19. Each variation of the drill consists of a flurry of strikes so that if one strike fails the practitioner is automatically following through without hesitation.
Vital Points	See Drills 18, 16 and 20.
Unbalancing	See Drills 18, 16 and 20.
Adrenaline Tolerant	Yes. See Drills 18, 16 and 20. The rehearsal of Drills in unfamiliar game stages until they are natural increases their adrenaline tolerance.
Low Maintenance	Yes.
Transferable skills	This drill provides a controlled opportunity to apply sequences from previous drills in an alternative tactical environment, as a result it directly promotes the transfer of skills.

Advanced points

The punching attacks in the assisted inside forearm receiver should aim to connect with LV 14. Once students have mastered the rigid forms of the drills as laid out above on both sides, they should then practice initiating the drills unpredictably, the attacker alone knowing whether he will start with a shove, punch, grab or grab/punch. Once students have become accustomed to this the next stage is to allow a range of unpredictability using the Sandan methods at the spear hand stage of the drills. The following stage should be the incorporation of Nidan movements into the drills, for example when the spear hand strike is palmed to the inside, Blue could easily respond with:

Any of the set basic drills outlined above.

Drill 13 – opposite side. A reverse inside receiver, front kick and cross combination from Heian Nidan.

Drill 12 – opposite side. Stepping in with a right knife hand receiver followed by a bicep attack, elbow strike, push and renewed attempt at a spear hand strike.

Drill 20 – opposite side.

Once this level of confidence is achieved there is no reason why White should not choose to attempt to attack with a punch immediately after grabbing Blue's intended hammerfist rather than just waiting to be locked or thrown. Similarly White could throw a punch immediately after diverting the spear hand strike, or even palm it from inside to outside and launch his own inside receiver, front kick and cross combination, or knife hand receiver combination. There is more than enough here for students to work upon. Whenever the techniques get messy it is important for the instructor to take the students back to isolated techniques to ensure that correct application of individual techniques are not substituted for brute strength once speed and unpredictability come into the equation. Occasionally, practicing the techniques slowly paired up at triple the distance (so no contact is actually made) can often give students greater opportunity to analyse whether they are making best use of their stances and hips. It also leads to a greater ability to visualise an opponent – an essential part of solo training.

As a general rule I am opposed to stepping back. In earlier drills defenders are encouraged to shift sideways or step in as a response to an attack. These defences are taught first so that they become the most natural behaviour. The step back here in the Sandan Drills and in Drill 13 reflect the fact that it is a common response under assault, therefore we as martial artists must be prepared to follow through and move into a retreating person.

Heian Yondan

The kata movements

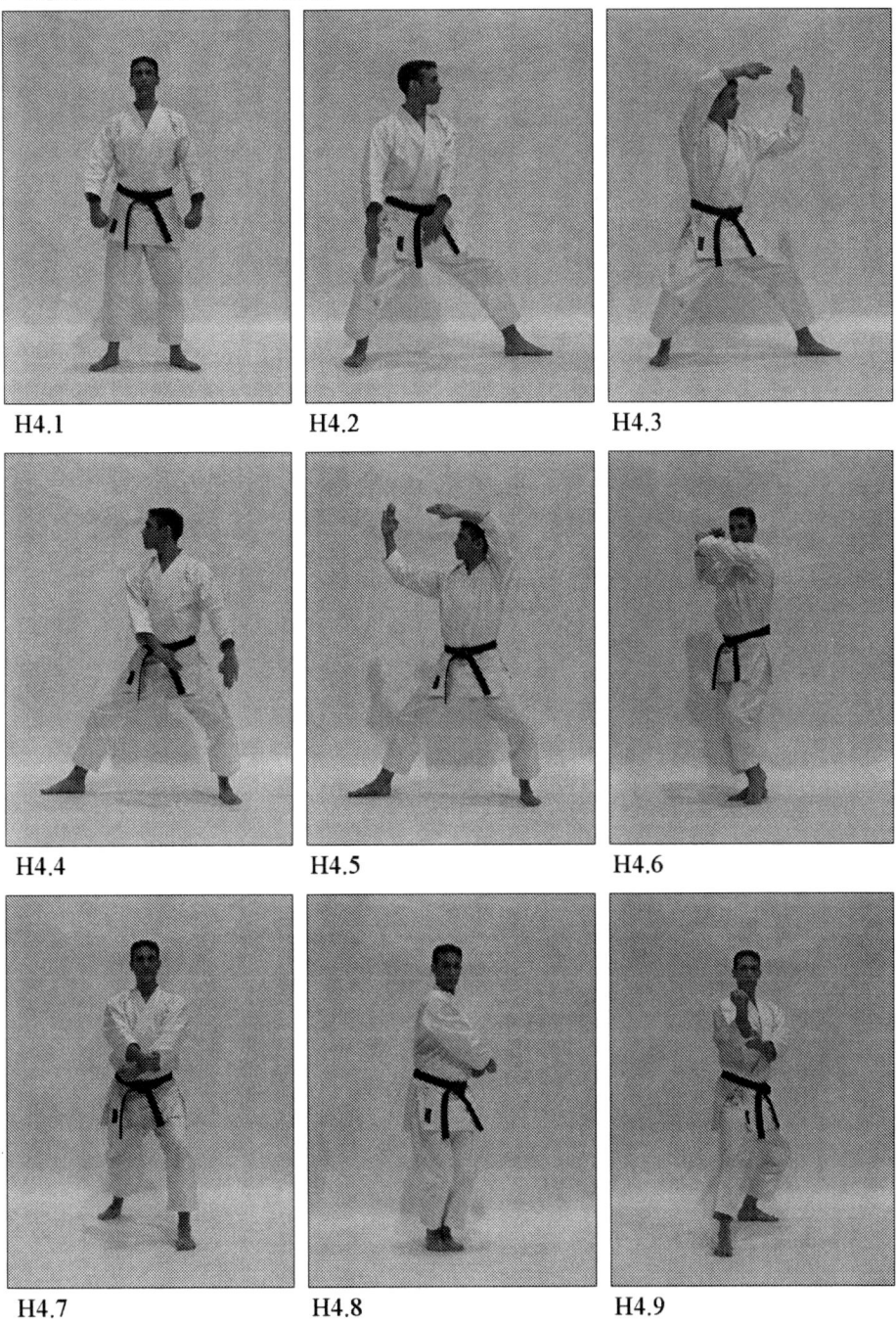

H4.1 H4.2 H4.3
H4.4 H4.5 H4.6
H4.7 H4.8 H4.9

Heian Yondan

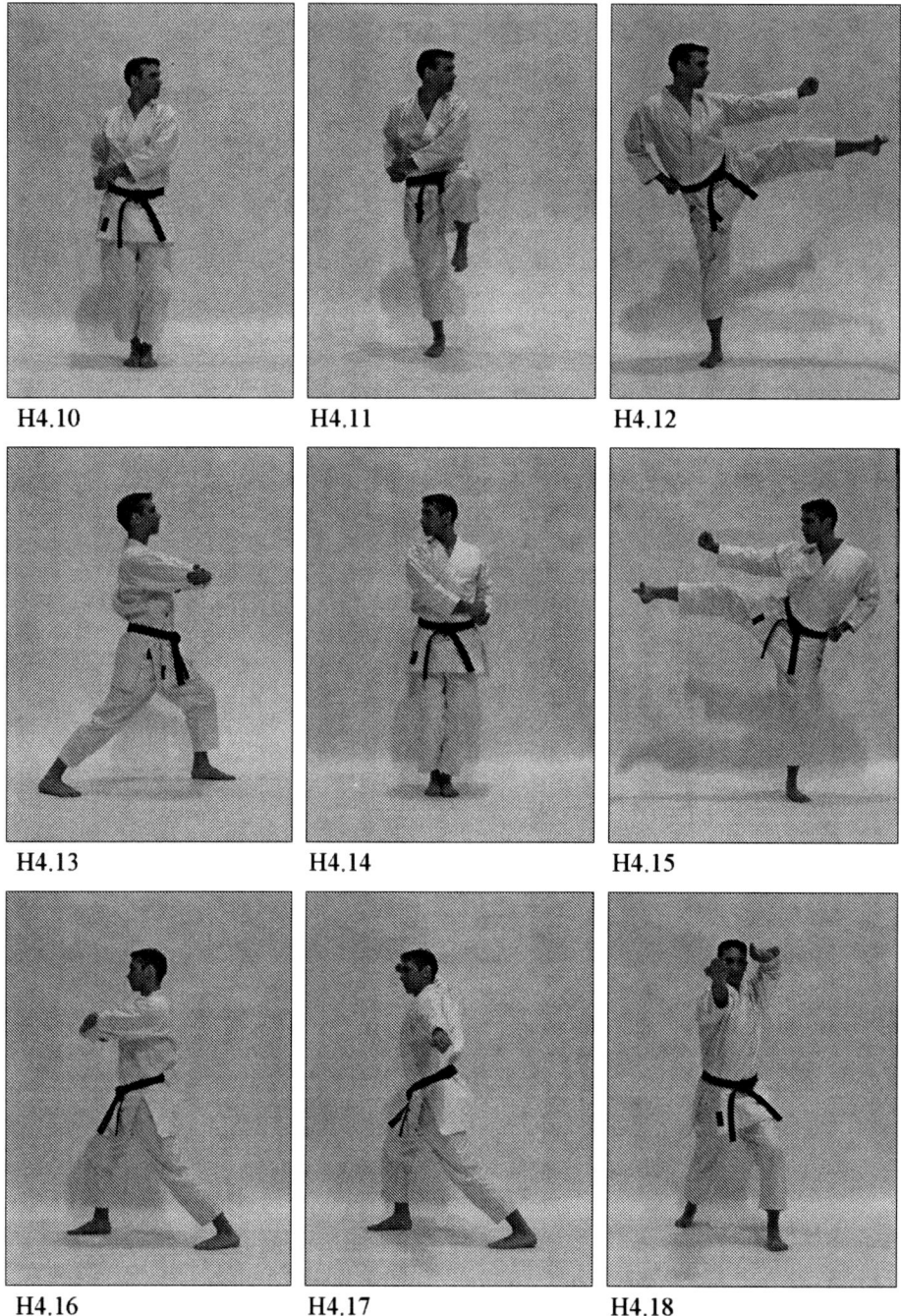

H4.10   H4.11   H4.12

H4.13   H4.14   H4.15

H4.16   H4.17   H4.18

Heian Yondan

H4.19　　　　　H4.20　　　　　H4.21

H4.22　　　　　H4.23　　　　　H4.24

H4.25　　　　　H4.26　　　　　H4.27

Heian Yondan

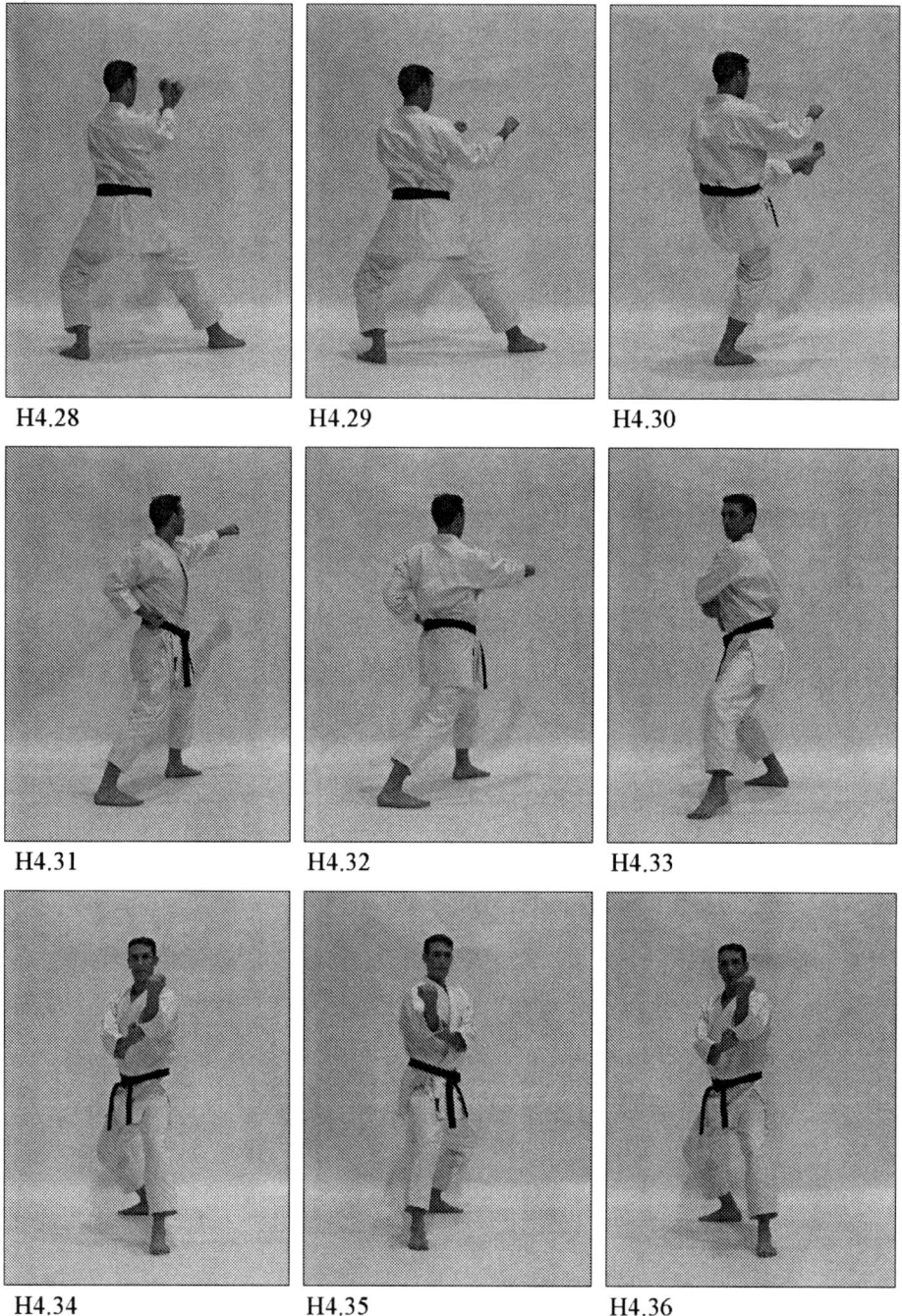

H4.28　　　H4.29　　　H4.30

H4.31　　　H4.32　　　H4.33

H4.34　　　H4.35　　　H4.36

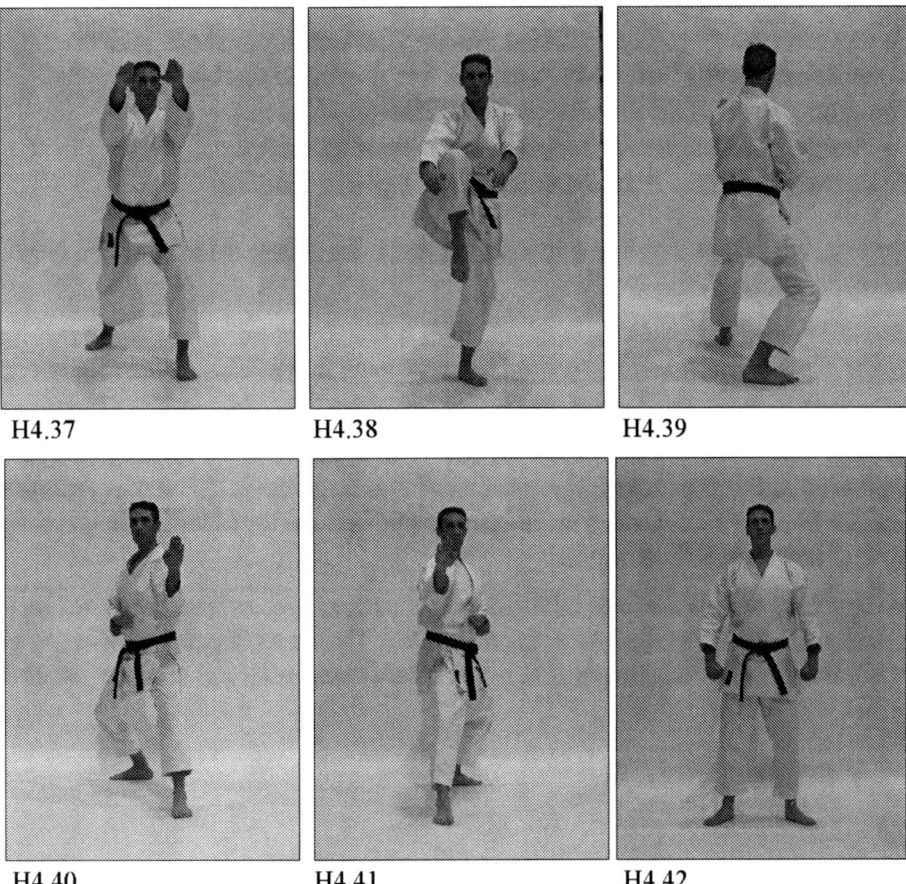

H4.37   H4.38   H4.39

H4.40   H4.41   H4.42

Training rationale

Please note that all drills should be practiced on both sides, however students should give prominence to defending from their habitual fence. To ensure a level of realism and technique flow, when struck practitioners are asked to simulate a 50-70% successful blow, thus folding over in response to punches or head strikes but not dropping completely as per a knockout. This allows students to train to follow through naturally from one technique into another with a more realistic body position that is not provided by a purely rigid training partner. In many instances these people make a remarkable recovery midway through the drills, but this serves to keep both practitioners on their toes. The simulation of the body's reaction to actual strikes also teaches students about how the body is likely to move, serves as mental preparation for real events and improves visualisation skills.

The Yondan drills supplement the core of self defence applications provided by the preceding drills in two ways; firstly by providing different methods of applying previously learnt techniques with alternative redundancy patterns, and secondly by introducing new techniques to negate alternative HAOV.

The purpose of the Heian Yondan drills is as follows:

- To provide students with alternative pre-emptive striking methods with multiple redundancy patterns that can be used in a free flowing situation.
- To introduce new HAOV and appropriate counter-measures.
- To introduce techniques for controlling grounded attackers.
- To increase the element of unpredictability in paired training.

Changes to the kata movement in the Heian Flow System

Sequences of movements are either initiated from a fence or a middle or end game fighting position instead of/ in addition to the preceding movement in the Kata. Some sequences begin from movements found in previous stages in the Heian set.

The side snap kick and backfist technique has been replaced by a kicking and punching technique that more closely reflects the movement illustrated by Gichin Funakoshi in *Karate Jutsu*. The line of movement for this technique has also been changed to enable it to follow the preceding application in a fluid manner.

The cross legged stance has not been retained in applications against standing attackers since it provides less stability than other stances available. The cross legged position is utilised however when the same finishing position is demonstrated with the attacker prone on the ground.

Heian Yondan drills

Drill 24

White approaches Blue from behind and attempts to control Blue by applying a full nelson hold (Pic 4.24.1).

Pic 4.24.1

Blue immediately drops his arms, turning them so that his thumbs point to the rear. At the same time Blue drops his weight to the right (Pic 4.24.2). Blue now reaches across to his left chest with his right hand and takes hold of White's fingers so that both hands are inside to inside and Blue's thumb is upward, for maximum effect Blue should ensure that White's little finger is pulled across the back across to the index finger (Pic 4.24.3). Blue now rotates his hand so that his thumb points downwards while raising his right arm so that the forearm is just above his forehead, this may not be fully possible due to the flexibility of some partners (Pic 4.24.4).

Pic 4.24.2
(H4.2)

Pic 4.24.3
(H4.3)

Pic 4.24.4
(H4.3)

Note that the blade of Blue's right hand must be in line with his forearm and not tilted upwards, otherwise insufficient pressure is placed on White's fingers. This pivots White from behind Blue to Blue's left hand side and Blue strikes White's head with the back of his left hand or forearm (Pic 4.24.5). As White slumps Blue follows through by grabbing White's neck and head with both raised hands and stepping forward with his right leg bringing both hands down in front of him to throw White over his shoulder (Pic 4.24.6).

Heian Yondan

Pic 4.24.5 (H4.3)   Pic 4.24.6 (H4.6)   Pic 4.24.7 (H4.7)

Only experienced throwers and breakfallers should attempt this technique. If White lands in a seated position and Blue has not let go, Blue can now step forward with one of his legs to push his knee into the centre of White's back while simultaneously turning his right fist so that it grinds into the left hand side of White's neck (Pic 4.24.7).

Effectiveness	**Comment**
HAOV	This is not a common attack but in recorded violent crime it seems to be more commonly used against women by men as an initial restraint prior to removal from an area and then assault. It is more likely to be used by security at night clubs or bars as a control prior to removal from the premises.
Multiplicity	The initial phases of this drill can be used as an open handed alternative to the opening stages of Drill 8 with the downward motion of the hands being used to break the grip as an initial defence with the redundancy of the raising of both arms as a follow up in the event of the punch (the left arm intercepting the right punch while the right hand palm strikes the jaw to the assailant's right).

Effectiveness	Comment
Predictable Response	This drill makes use of the predictable response to the finger lock applied by the right hand. The clockwise movement of the attacker in a response to try and alleviate the pain is anticipated by the striking movement of the left hand.
Initiative	This drill is reactive rather than proactive, but it trains practitioners to regain the initiative from a compromising situation.
Redundancy	Once the attacker has been struck the throw and strangle provide redundancies, however there is no built in redundancy for the movements leading up to this stage. In the event of a failure to apply the finger lock possible options may be kicking techniques backwards to the shin and reverse head butts. These may allow the gripping of the attacker's left hand/wrist by the practitioner's right, a small counter clockwise pivot to enable a facing position and then Drills 1,3 or 4 may be employed. Once this Drill is employed in the random situation provided by Heian Sandan, such failures will be likely for a time and thus these alternatives may be developed further.
Vital Points	Potential strikes to the ear and ST 5.
Unbalancing	Potential to unbalance from above by both the finger lock and the head throw. Potential to unbalance from below through shin kicking.
Adrenaline Tolerant	With practice this technique can become adrenaline tolerant, however unless it is drilled regularly the finger locking technique is likely to fail under the influence of adrenaline.

Effectiveness	Comment
Low Maintenance	No. The Drill requires regular practice. This is a weakness since it is designed to combat an attack that is not particularly likely to occur.
Transferable skills	The redundancies make use of skills in other drills, but the core of this Drill makes no real use of transferable skills other than situational awareness.

Drill 25

White grabs Blue's lapel (Pic 4.25.1).

Pic 4.25.1
(H4.8)

Blue attacks White pre-emptively, stepping forward with his right leg (keeping his weight on his left for stability) to the outside of White, striking White's extended forearm with an inward motion of his right arm (Pic 4.25.2) before extending it outwards in an inside receiver to strike White's right temple (Pic 4.25.3). Blue's left hand simultaneously either grabs White's left forearm or uppercuts into White's ribs.

Pic 4.25.2
(H4.9)

Pic 4.25.3
(H4.9)

This should drop White, but for the purposes of the drill Blue is trained to follow though anticipating failure by flowing from one strike automatically into the next.

Blue follows through by retracting his left fist towards his hip, drawing White's relaxed hand to that level and retracting his extended right hand to his right hip to control the back of White's left wrist. At the same time Blue withdraws his extended right leg so that it is just behind his left, enabling his left leg to protect his groin (Pic 4.25.4). Blue then applies a rolling downward motion to White's hand to apply pressure to either the tendons of the back of the hand or the wrist, forcing White to the ground in a wrist lock (Pic 4.25.5).

Pic 4.25.4
(H4.10)

Pic 4.25.5
(H4.22)

Heian Yondan

With White on his back as a result of the wrist lock and Blue still gripping and pulling upwards on his left hand (this can follow any throw executed so far where control of the arm has been maintained), Blue kicks White's temple with his right foot and pushes between White's shoulder blades with his left shin (Pic 4.25.6). Blue applies pressure on White's chin as he steps over and pulls the back of White's left elbow across his right thigh (Pic 4.25.7). Blue tucks his left leg behind his right, sandwiching White's neck and raising his left heel to apply increased pressure while increasing pressure on White's wrist with his hands (Pic 4.25.8).

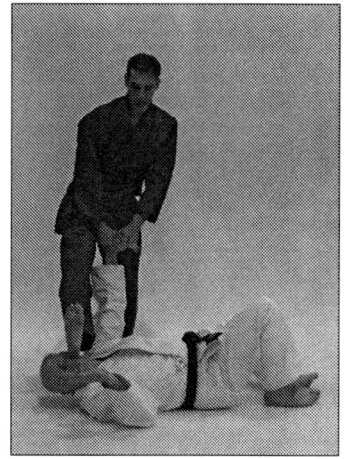
Pic 4.25.6
(H4.22)

Pic 4.25.7
(H4.22)

Pic 4.25.8
(H4.22)

Effectiveness	Comment
HAOV	A one handed front clothing grab followed by a punch to the head is one of the most commonly recorded attacks.
Multiplicity	This drill can be used pre-emptively without any grab either to initiate a fight or from a free position in a mid-game situation. Almost identical movements are used to the inside in Drill 18 and its redundancy drills. It thus scores highly here since it can be used both reactively and proactively, inside and outside.

Effectiveness	Comment
Predictable Response	This drill anticipates the likely body movement following each strike and follows through with a technique appropriate to the target position.
Initiative	This drill scores highly since although it responds to a grab, it is proactive in not waiting for any subsequent percussive technique. Once the drill begins it maintains the initiative with a flurry of strikes to multiple targets at different levels to confuse, disorientate and disable the attacker. The techniques of this drill may also be used proactively without waiting for any lapel grab.
Redundancy	This drill works on the assumption that the initial strike has failed to drop the attacker. As a result the tactic is then changed by an immediate wrist lock follow up to control the attacker and put him on the ground. If this is insufficient to control the attacker then a further redundancy consisting of kicking techniques, an arm control and a strangle is practised. Drills 26 and 27 provide redundancies and alternatives to the wrist lock.
Vital Points	Potential strikes to GB 32, LV 14, ear, ST 5, ST 3, GB 1, GB 2, mind point and BL 49, 50 and 51.
Unbalancing	Potential unbalancing from above via strike to the ear and wrist lock.
Adrenaline Tolerant	Yes. The techniques used are simple and easy to execute. To execute this drill it is important that the practitioner recognises that a grab is a physical attack that requires an immediate response.

Effectiveness	Comment
Low Maintenance	Moderate. The initial movements of this drill are so common throughout the Heian Flow System that they are very low maintenance. The wrist lock is simple but I would advise considerable practice before using it safely under pressurised conditions (safe for your partner, not for you).
Transferable skills	This drill utilises techniques (and entire sequences) already developed in preceding drills. Its techniques are used in many subsequent drills.

Drill 26

White grabs Blue's lapel with his left hand (Pic 4.26.1).

Pic 4.26.1
(H4.8)

Blue attacks White pre-emptively, stepping forward with his right leg (keeping his weight on his left for stability) to the outside of White, striking White's extended forearm with an inward motion of his right arm (Pic 4.26.2) before extending it outwards in an inside receiver to strike White's right temple (Pic 4.26.3). Blue's left hand simultaneously either grabs White's left forearm or uppercuts into White's ribs.

Pic 4.26.2
(H4.9)

Pic 4.26.3
(H4.9)

This should drop White, but for the purposes of the drill Blue is trained to follow though anticipating failure flowing from one strike automatically into the next.

Blue follows through by retracting his left fist to his hip, drawing White's relaxed hand to that level and retracting his extended right hand to his right hip to control the back of White's left wrist. At the same time Blue withdraws his extended right leg so that it is just behind his left, enabling his left leg to protect his groin. Blue then applies a rolling downward motion to White's hand to apply pressure to either the tendons of the back of the hand or the wrist, forcing White to the ground in a wrist lock (Pic 4.26.4) (note that this technique has been pulled short in the picture to avoid breaking White's wrist).

Releasing the pressure on White's wrist, Blue allows White to rise as if the lock has been incorrectly applied or has had no effect. Blue promptly kicks White with his left leg at either the inside knee (Sp 10) or the groin (to bring White's head forward) (Pic 4.26.5) and then punches White in the face with his left hand (Pic 4.26.6). Imagining that this has still not dropped White, Blue extends his left hand to grasp the back of White's neck and, stepping forward with his left leg, Blue pulls White's head towards him with his left hand while he attacks the same target with his right elbow (Pic 4.26.7).

Heian Yondan

Pic 4.26.4
(H4.10)

Pic 4.26.5
(H4.12)

Pic 4.26.6
(H4.12)

Pic 4.26.7
(H4.13)

Effectiveness	Comment
HAOV	A one handed front clothing grab followed by a punch to the head is one of the most commonly recorded attacks.

Effectiveness	Comment
Multiplicity	This drill can be used pre-emptively without any grab either to initiate a fight or from a free position in a mid-game situation. Almost identical movements are used to the inside in Drill 18 and its redundancy drills. It thus scores highly here since it can be used both reactively and proactively, inside and outside in either opening game, mid game or end game situations.
Predictable Response	This drill anticipates the likely body movement following each strike and follows through with a technique appropriate to the target position.
Initiative	This drill scores highly since although it responds to a grab, it is proactive in not waiting for any subsequent percussive technique. Once the drill begins it maintains the initiative with a flurry of strikes to multiple targets at different levels to confuse, disorientate and disable the attacker. The techniques of this drill may also be used proactively without waiting for any lapel grab.
Redundancy	This drill is essentially a redundancy for Drill 24. At each level failure is anticipated and an appropriate back up technique rehearsed.
Vital Points	Potential strikes to GB 32, LV 14, ear, ST 5, ST 3, GB 1, GB 2, mind point, SP 10, genitalia, CO 19.
Unbalancing	Potential unbalancing from above via strikes to the ear and the wrist lock. Potential unbalancing from below via strikes to GB 32 and SP 10.

Heian Yondan

Effectiveness	Comment
Adrenaline Tolerant	Yes. The techniques used are simple and easy to execute. To execute this drill it is important that the practitioner recognises that a grab is a physical attack that requires an immediate response.
Low Maintenance	Yes.
Transferable skills	This Drill uses skills developed in preceding drills and mimics the movements of other drills in many other ways.

Drill 27

White grabs Blue's right lapel/upper arm/shoulder with his left hand (Pic 4.27.1).

Pic 4.27.1

Blue attacks White pre-emptively, stepping forward with his left leg (keeping his weight on his right for stability) to the inside of White, striking with an inside receiver to White's left temple. Blue's right hand simultaneously uppercuts into White's ribs (Pic 4.27.2).

Pic 4.27.2
(H4.36)

This should drop White, but for the purposes of the drill Blue is trained to follow though anticipating failure flowing from one strike automatically into the next. Rather than moving to the biceps and sternum strikes Blue reaches forward with his left hand to grab White's right ear while moving his right hand round to grab White's left ear (or the back of White's neck – pressure applied to the temples with the thumbs assists this move, without psychological training you are unlikely to be able to thumb the eyes) (Pic 4.27.3).

Pic 4.27.3   Pic 4.27.4
(H4.37)   (H4.38)

Blue now pulls down with both hands as he simultaneously raises his right knee into White's chest or face (note that if White resists the pull Blue's leg can extend into a kick to the genitals)

(Pic 4.27.4). White then turns to step down backwards (as if to face another threat) with his right leg into White (Pic 4.27.5), striking White with his right elbow as he extends his right hand into a fence in the opposite direction (Pic 4.27.6).

Pic 4.27.5
(H4.38)

Pic 4.27.6
(H4.39)

Effectiveness	Comment
HAOV	A one handed front clothing grab followed by a punch to the head is one of the most commonly recorded attacks.
Multiplicity	This drill can be used pre-emptively without any grab either to initiate a fight or from a free position in a mid-game situation. Almost identical movements are used to the inside in Drill 18 and its redundancy drills. It thus scores highly here since it can be used both reactively and proactively, inside and outside in either opening game, mid game or end game situations.
Predictable Response	This drill anticipates the likely body movement following each strike and follows through with a technique appropriate to the target position.

Effectiveness	Comment
Initiative	This drill scores highly since although it responds to a grab, it is proactive in not waiting for any subsequent percussive technique. Once the drill begins it maintains the initiative with a flurry of strikes to multiple targets at different levels to confuse, disorientate and disable the attacker. The techniques of this drill may also be used proactively without waiting for any lapel grab.
Redundancy	This drill acts as an alternative redundancy for Drill 22. The elbow strike (and potential kick with the step down) act as a redundancy for an ineffective (or resisted) knee strike which in turn acts as a redundancy for the initial grab/strike or two handed strike.
Vital Points	Potential strikes to SP 10, LV 14, ear, ST 5, ST 3, GB 1, GB 2, mind point, SP 10, genitalia, CO 19.
Unbalancing	Potential unbalancing from above via strike to the ear or the head pull and strike. Potential unbalancing from below via stepping strikes to SP 10 and kick to the genitalia.
Adrenaline Tolerant	Yes. This drill works with the natural reaction to grab an attacker.
Low Maintenance	Yes.
Transferable skills	Yes. This drill utilizes previously rehearsed skills and adds a finishing technique (the head grab and knee strike) that can be added onto almost all of the Heian Drills.

Drill 28
White grabs Blue (Pic 4.28.1).

Pic 4.28.1

Blue attacks White pre-emptively with a left augmented inside receiver (Pic 4.28.2). Blue follows through with a strike to the bicep (Pic 4.28.3) and an elbow attack to Whites's sternum, but this time Blue fails to move White backwards (Pic 4.28.4). Blue drops his left arm to strike into the left hand side of White's abdomen with a down sweep and punches straight over the top of this with a right downward angled punch (Pic 4.28.5). Blue then grabs and pulls White's jacket with his left hand as he steps forward with his right leg into White, executing a right inside receiver to the right hand side of White's neck, strangling him (Pic 4.28.6).

Pic 4.28.2 (H3.11)   Pic 4.28.3 (H3.12)   Pic 4.28.4 (H3.12)

Pic 4.28.5 (H4.7)   Pic 4.28.6 (H4.9)

Effectiveness	Comment
HAOV	A one handed front clothing grab followed by a punch to the head is one of the most commonly recorded attacks.
Multiplicity	This drill can be used pre-emptively without any grab either to initiate a fight or from a free position in a mid-game situation. Almost identical movements are used to the inside in Drill 18 and its redundancy drills. It thus scores highly here since it can be used both reactively and proactively, inside and outside in either opening game, mid game or end game situations.
Predictable Response	This drill anticipates the likely body movement following each strike and follows through with a technique appropriate to the target position. The drill also anticipates the 'unpredictable response' of the strike to the sternum failing to move the attacker.

Effectiveness	Comment
Initiative	This drill scores highly since although it responds to a grab, it is proactive in not waiting for any subsequent percussive technique. Once the drill begins it maintains the initiative with a flurry of strikes to multiple targets at different levels to confuse, disorientate and disable the attacker. The techniques of this drill may also be used proactively without waiting for any lapel grab.
Redundancy	This drill is a redundancy for Drill 18. A sequence of possible options following the failure of this redundancy are trained in Drill 35.
Vital Points	Potential strikes to SP 10, LV 14, LV 13, CV 14, ST 5, ST 3, mind point, GB 1, GB 2, ear, CO 18, SI 17, LU 5, Bicep.
Unbalancing	Potential unbalancing from above via strikes to the ear and to the sternum. Potential unbalancing from below via stepping strike to SP 10.
Adrenaline Tolerant	Yes.
Low Maintenance	Yes.
Transferable skills	Yes. Uses previously rehearsed movements.

Drill 29

White approaches Blue from the rear and places his left hand on Blue's left shoulder with his left leg forward (Pic 4.29.1).

Pic 4.29.1
(H4.17)

Blue swings his left arm upwards to strike the outside of White's left triceps, pivoting his body in a counter-clockwise direction (and turning White clockwise) so that he is facing White offline (Pic 4.29.2). Blue then slides back his left arm towards the left hand side of his head, gripping and pulling White's left forearm as Blue simultaneously strikes White's extended elbow joint with a right knife hand strike (Pic 4.29.3).

Pic 4.29.2   Pic 4.29.3   Pic 4.29.4
(H4.18)   (H4.18)   (H4.19)

Blue then kicks the back of White's exposed left hamstring with his rear (right) leg, causing White to collapse in front of him with his back to him (Pic 4.29.4). As Blue steps down from his kick he brings his right arm down to strike into the back right hand side of White's neck, this is followed by a similar quick motion with his left hand which slaps down on the left hand side of White's neck (Pics 4.29.5 and 4.29.6). Blue then strikes in, up and back with both fists to White's temples, applying continuous pressure with his fists while his forearms apply pressure to both sides of White's neck while his right knee presses into White's back (Pic 4.29.7).

Pic 4.29.5   Pic 4.29.6   Pic 4.29.7
(H4.20)   (H4.21)   (H4.22)

Effectiveness	Comment
HAOV	Not in the top 10 recorded HAOV though an approach experienced by the author. The rear grab is perhaps more common against those who have taken a degree of time to build up indignation against a real or imagined slight.
Multiplicity	As can be seen in Drill 30 the defensive sequence can be used effectively (though striking different targets) whichever arm or hand the attacker leads with. The defence can be used for both a lower or upper arm grab in addition to a shoulder grab.

Effectiveness	Comment
Predictable Response	The drill works within the expected dangers of the position and anticipates through its techniques the vulnerabilities for both attacker and defender. The follow through techniques anticipate the pattern of movement induced by the initial strikes.
Initiative	This sequence attempts to take the initiative back by moving offline to avoid the expected strike. The initiative is then kept through a flurry of strikes at multiple levels and angles.
Redundancy	The use of multiple strikes ensures that if one fails the defender is already prepared and trained to follow through with another technique. The drill can also be used in an alternative mid or opening game situation in response to an upper level punch.
Vital Points	Potential strikes to TH 11, BL 37, strangle.
Unbalancing	Unbalancing from above from over-extending B's left arm and striking to TH 11. Unbalancing from below through striking to BL 37.
Adrenaline Tolerant	Yes. Works with the natural instinct to grab and control. All the strikes use broad sweeping movements and the kick is low level.
Low Maintenance	Yes, due to its simplicity.
Transferable skills	Yes. Utilises kicking skills developed in earlier drills and refines accuracy.

Drill 30

White approaches Blue from the rear and places his right hand on Blue's left shoulder (Pic 4.30.1).

Pic 4.30.1
(H4.17)

Blue spins round striking out with first his left and then his right in the same motion used in the previous drill.

Variation 1. White has not had time to throw a punch. Blue makes contact with White's left bicep and pulls on this left arm as his right hand strikes into White's neck (Pic 4.30.2).

 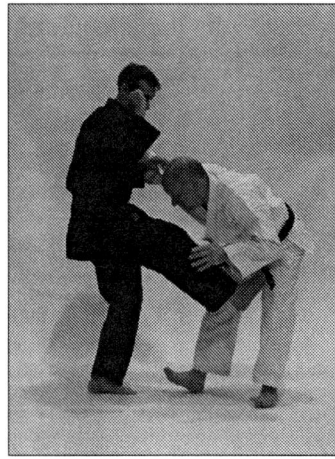 

Pic 4.30.2 Pic 4.30.3 Pic 4.30.4
(H4.18)   (H4.19)   (H4.20)

Keeping hold of White's left arm, Blue kicks White's genitals with his rear (right) leg (Pic 4.30.3) and as he steps down slaps the back of White's neck with the heel of his right hand so that White is bent double facing Blue (Pic 4.30.4). Blue's left hand then strikes down onto White in an identical motion (care must be taken near the spine) (Pic 4.30.5). In this instance, given White's low position, Blue strikes down with his right forearm as his left fist punches into White's neck (Pic 4.30.6).

Pic 4.30.5
(H4.21)

Pic 4.30.6
(H4.22)

Variation 2. White begins to throw the punch but Blue's turning strike to White's left bicep stalls its momentum and power (Pic 4.30.7).

Pic 4.30.7
(H4.17)

Pic 4.30.8
(H4.18)

Pic 4.30.9
(H4.19)

Heian Yondan

Blue's right hand strike palms aside the weakened punch (Pic 4.30.8). Blue kicks White in the genitals with his right leg (Pic 4.30.9). Blue then strikes down onto the back of White's neck with his right hand (Pic 4.30.10), followed by his left (Pic 4.30.11). Blue then finishes White with a double forearm hammer strike to both of White's temples (Pic 4.30.12). If B punched with a cross and his left leg back, A's kick will catch B in the genitals and the follow through will be as per variation 1.

Pic 4.30.10
(H4.20)

Pic 4.30.11
(H4.21)

Pic 4.30.12
(H4.22)

Pic 4.30.13
(H4.17)

Pic 4.30.14
(H4.18)

Pic 4.30.15
(H4.19)

Variation 3. White's punch is either i) not significantly affected by Blue's bicep strike (which may have retracted out of range due to the speed of the punch) or ii) is already so advanced that Blue has not had time to strike the bicep.

Blue swings his right arm upward to deflect the punch, striking B's left arm with his right forearm (Pic 4.30.13). Blue immediately lashes out with a kick to White's genitals (Pic 4.20.14) and two palm strikes to White's neck (Pic 4.30.15 and 4.30.16). On this occasion White's body position lends itself to a right uppercut while the left hand grabs (Pic 4.30.17).

Pic 4.30.16　　　　　　　　Pic 4.30.17
(H4.20)　　　　　　　　　(H4.22)

Blue swings his left arm upwards to catch the underside of White's punching arm (Pic 4.30.18). Blue then strikes into White's triceps with his right hand (Pic 4.30.19). Blue then kicks White in the exposed thigh (Pic 4.30.20). Blue follows through with two downward strikes as before (Pics 4.30.21 and 4.30.22). Due to White's advanced collapse Blue extends his right hand into a punch to White's temple as he goes down (Pic 4.30.23).

Heian Yondan

Pic 4.30.18
(H4.17)

Pic 4.30.19
(H4.18)

Pic 4.30.20
(H4.19)

Pic 4.30.21
(H4.20)

Pic 4.30.22
(H4.21)

Pic 4.30.23
(H4.22)

Effectiveness	Comment
HAOV	Not in the top 10 recorded HAOV though an approach experienced by the author. The rear grab is perhaps more common against those who have taken a degree of time to build up indignation against a real or imagined slight.
Multiplicity	As can be seen in the variations inherent in this drill (and Drill 26), the movements can be applied in a number of situations to good effect.
Predictable Response	The drill works within the expected dangers of the position and anticipates through its techniques the vulnerabilities for both attacker and defender. The follow through techniques anticipate the pattern of movement induced by the initial strikes.
Initiative	This sequence attempts to take the initiative back by moving offline to avoid the expected strike. The initiative is then kept through a flurry of strikes at multiple levels and angles.
Redundancy	The use of multiple strikes ensures that if one fails the defender is already prepared and trained to follow through with another technique. The drill can also be used in an alternative mid or opening game situation in response to an upper level punch.
Vital Points	Potential strikes to HT 2, GB 32, ST 9, CO 18, SI 16, SI 17, ST 5, GB 2, GB 1, ear, mind point, control at Lu 7, genitalia, strangle.
Unbalancing	Unbalancing from above through over-extending B's arm and from below with potential leg and genitalia strikes.

Effectiveness	Comment
Adrenaline Tolerant	Yes. Works with the natural instinct to grab and control. All the strikes use broad sweeping movements and the kick is low level.
Low Maintenance	Yes, due to its simplicity.
Transferable skills	Yes uses roughly identical movements in the same sequence as the preceding drill, develops situational awareness that can benefit the performance of all drills and improves the accuracy of low level kicking.

A note on Drills 29 and 30.

It is very important to do two things each time you turn in response:

- Duck.
- Ensure that your left arm and shoulder is curved and raised to protect your head.

Drill 31

White seizes both of Blue's lapels with both of his hands (Pic 4.31.1).

Pic 4.31.1

Anticipating either a head butt or a knee strike Blue immediately drops his weight back and down with his right leg while thrusting both his fists across the top and outside of White's forearms in front of his face and towards White's jaw Pic (4.31.2)(palms can be used instead). Blue then hammerfist strikes down and outward with both hands, striking either to White's collar bone, biceps or forearm (depending upon whether White had tried to head butt and thus how collapsed he is following the forward thrust) (Pic 4.31.3).

Taking advantage of the opening that this creates, Blue keeps hold of White with his extended arms and raises his knee for a strike or in preparation for a kick into White's genitals with his rear (right leg) (Pics 4.31.4 & 4.31.5). Stepping forward Blue attacks White with a jab and cross combination (Pics 4.31.6 & 4.31.7).

Pic 4.31.2
(H4.23)

Pic 4.31.3
(H4.24)

Pic 4.31.4
(H4.25)

Heian Yondan

Pic 4.31.5 (H4.25) Pic 4.31.6 (H4.26) Pic 4.31.7 (H4.27)

Effectiveness	Comment
HAOV	The double grab (or push) followed by a head butt is one of the most common forms of attack recorded.
Multiplicity	The techniques used in this drill can be used alternatively in response to a single arm grab or pre-emptively in a non-contact close proximity situation. The attack can also be used in close proximity in a mid game situation.
Predictable Response	This drill exploits the predictable movement of the head following a double grab with the interception of the fists, doubling the efficiency of the strike with no extra effort.

Effectiveness	Comment
Initiative	This drill initiates from a position of disadvantage and regains the initiative through nullifying the initial aggressive strike and with a potentially devastating counter strike and following through with a flurry of techniques. The drill can also be used to initiate conflict pre-emptively.
Redundancy	The drill uses multiple strikes so that if the initial strike fails the defender is trained to follow through without pause thus reducing the chance of losing the initiative. The step back further reduces the chances of the initial blow landing in the event that the initial strike is too slow to intercept the forward motion of the head directly (in which case it will catch the aggressor's ears leading to less damage overall but potentially a more incapacitated assailant). The kick can be employed at multiple ranges at either mid or low level.
Vital Points	Potential strikes to ST 5, mind point, ears, ST 9, CO 18, ST 12, CO 10, genitalia, SP 10.
Unbalancing	Potential unbalancing from above due to strikes to ears and CO 10 and from below via kick to either genitalia or SP 10.
Adrenaline Tolerant	Yes, works with the flinch reflex to put arms in front of face and duck down. Uses simple motor skills.
Low Maintenance	Yes.
Transferable skills	Works basic punching and kicking skills that can be employed in other drills.

Drill 32

Blue attempts a hammerfist strike to White which White deflects with a right palm as in Drills 20 and 21 (Pic 4.31.1).

Pic 4.32.1   Pic 4.32.2   Pic 4.32.3
(H3.15)   (H3.23)   (H3.23)

Blue strikes over the top of White's right arm with his right elbow (Pic 4.32.2).

As Blue attempts an S bend lock White raises his elbow above his wrist and pulls back with his arm, shoulder and hips (Pic 4.32.3).

White strikes Blue's temple with a knife hand strike (Pic 4.32.4).

Heian Yondan

Pic 4.32.4
(White H4.18)

Effectiveness	Comment
HAOV	The S bend lock is an uncommon technique overall.
Multiplicity	The techniques used in this drill can be used alternatively in response to an attack from behind or palming any straight punch to the side.
Predictable Response	This teaches a flinch reflex to the beginning movement of a high s bend lock.
Initiative	This drill teaches a method of regaining the initiative.
Redundancy	If the escape is not fully achieved the strike to the head ensures that it can be completed. The training of this sequence in an alternative scenario ensures that the practitioner will automatically keep striking.
Vital Points	Potential strikes to ST 5, mind point, ears, ST 9, CO 18, ST 12, genitalia, SP 10, GB 32.

Effectiveness	Comment
Unbalancing	Potential unbalancing from above due to strikes to ear/temple and CO 10 and from below via kick to either genitalia, GB 32 or SP 10.
Adrenaline Tolerant	Yes, works with the survival reflex to pull away.
Low Maintenance	Yes.
Transferable skills	Works basic punching and kicking skills that can be employed in other drills.

Advanced points

By this time students should be looking to strike and grab available vital points in the target areas indicated. Wherever possible steps to both the inside and outside leg should attack points at those points.

Once mastered, the defence against the full nelson hold can be incorporated into Drill 22 by Blue instead of the Chancery head lock with White applying the full nelson as Blue pivots and turns his back towards him. The lack of predictability here serves to sharpen responses to this attack.

In Drill 25, if the attacker grabs the right arm instead of the lapel then the grabbing arm can be treated like a punch and Drill 13 on the opposite side can be employed.

Once proficient in the variations presented here of the augmented inside receiver, students should attempt to apply them at random or preference to the techniques in Heian Sandan. This forces both training partners to maintained a heightened awareness during flow drill training.

Once proficiency has been attained in the defence against a double lapel grab, students can start defending against the jab and cross combination using moves learnt in the Nidan and Sandan stages of the Flow System.

Heian Godan

The kata movements

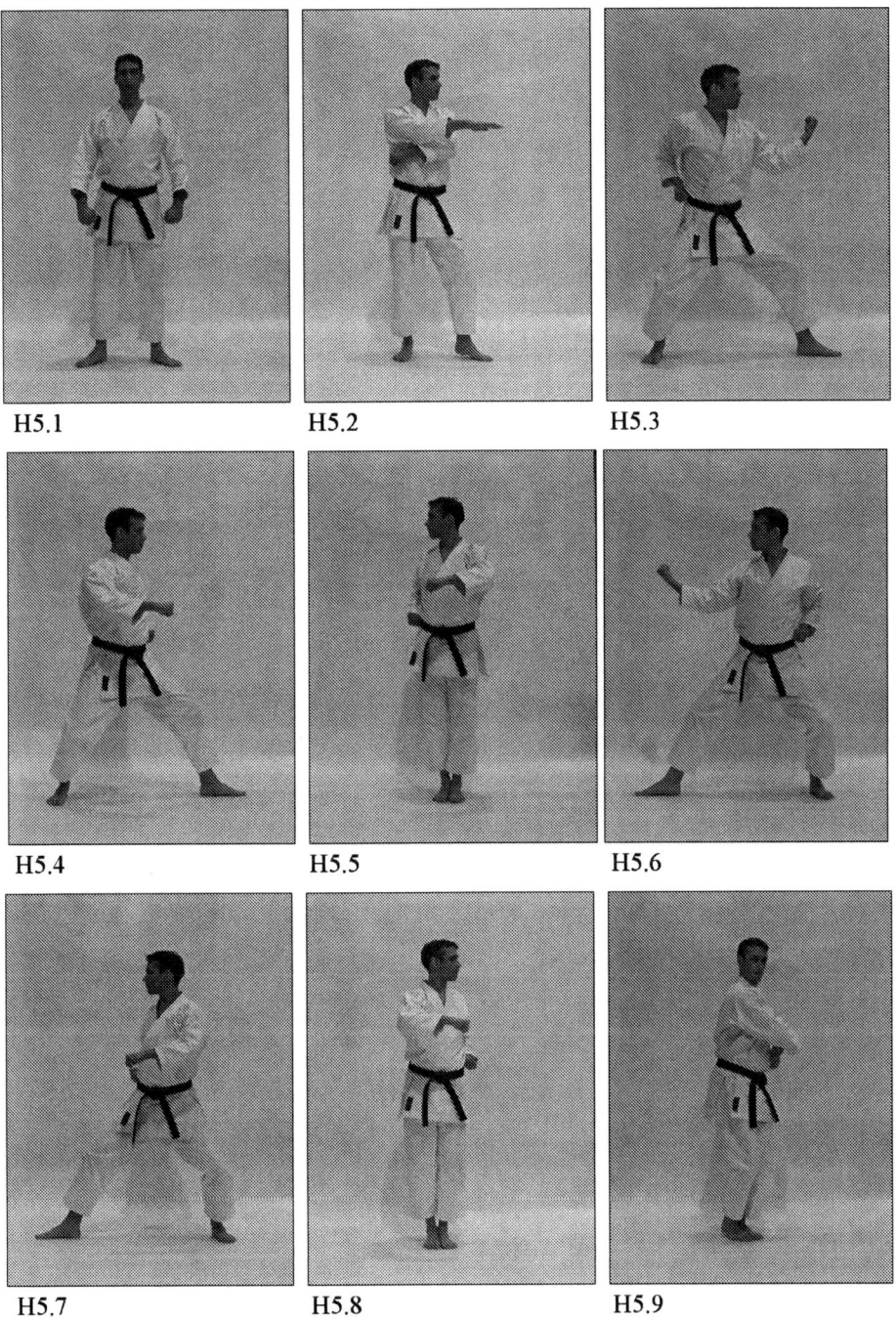

H5.1　　　　　　　　H5.2　　　　　　　　H5.3

H5.4　　　　　　　　H5.5　　　　　　　　H5.6

H5.7　　　　　　　　H5.8　　　　　　　　H5.9

Heian Godan

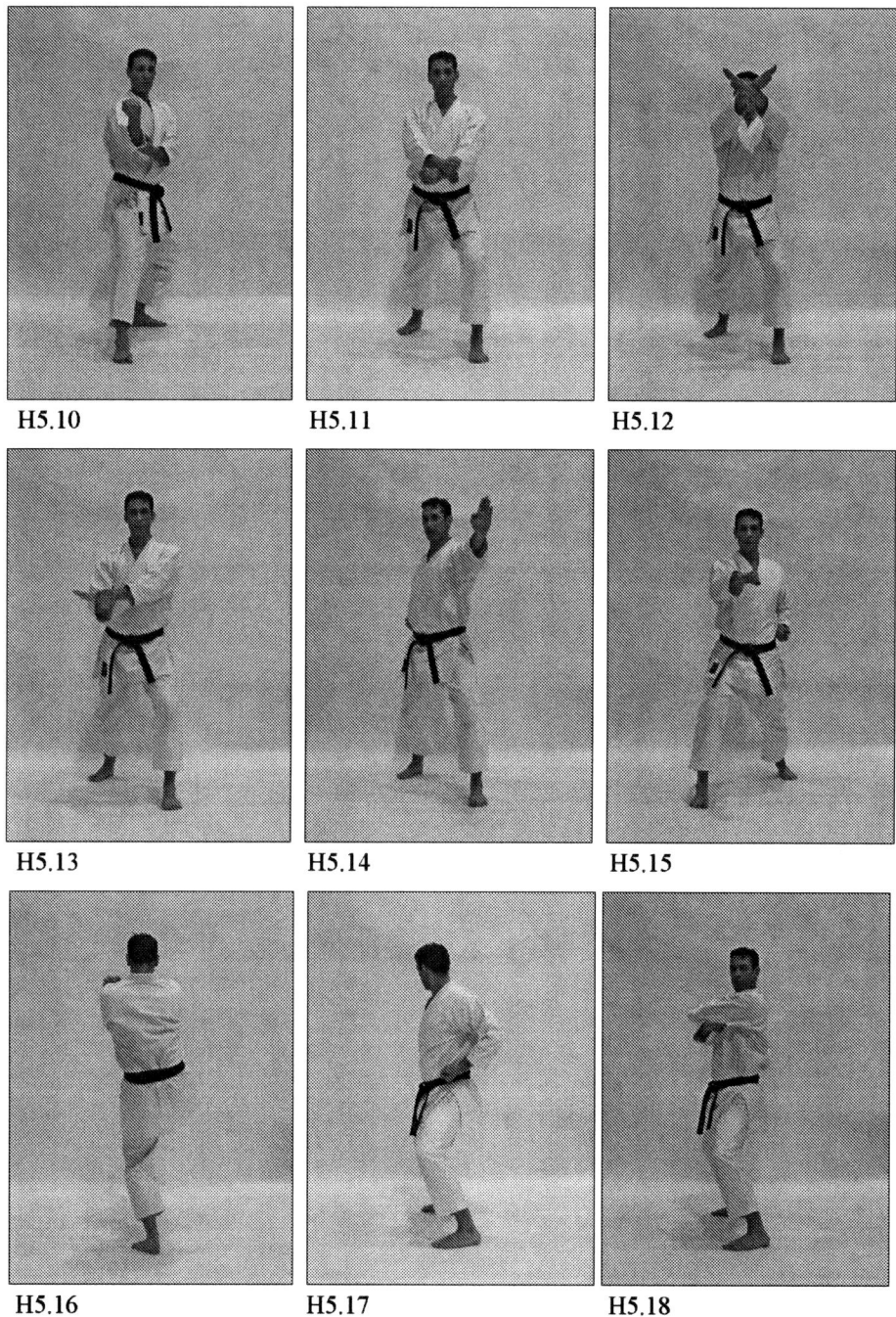

H5.10　　　　　　　H5.11　　　　　　　H5.12

H5.13　　　　　　　H5.14　　　　　　　H5.15

H5.16　　　　　　　H5.17　　　　　　　H5.18

Heian Godan

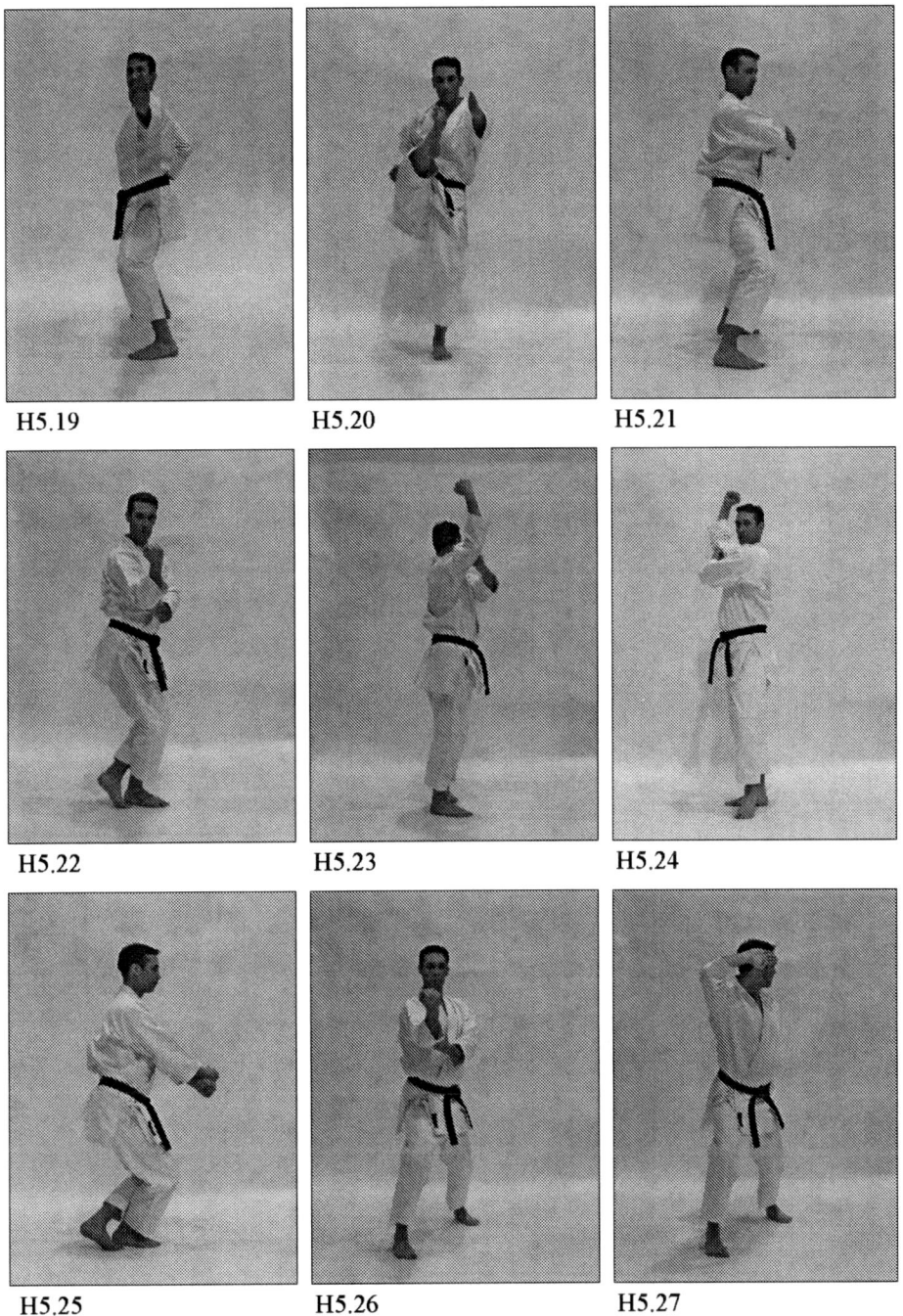

H5.19　　　　H5.20　　　　H5.21

H5.22　　　　H5.23　　　　H5.24

H5.25　　　　H5.26　　　　H5.27

Heian Godan

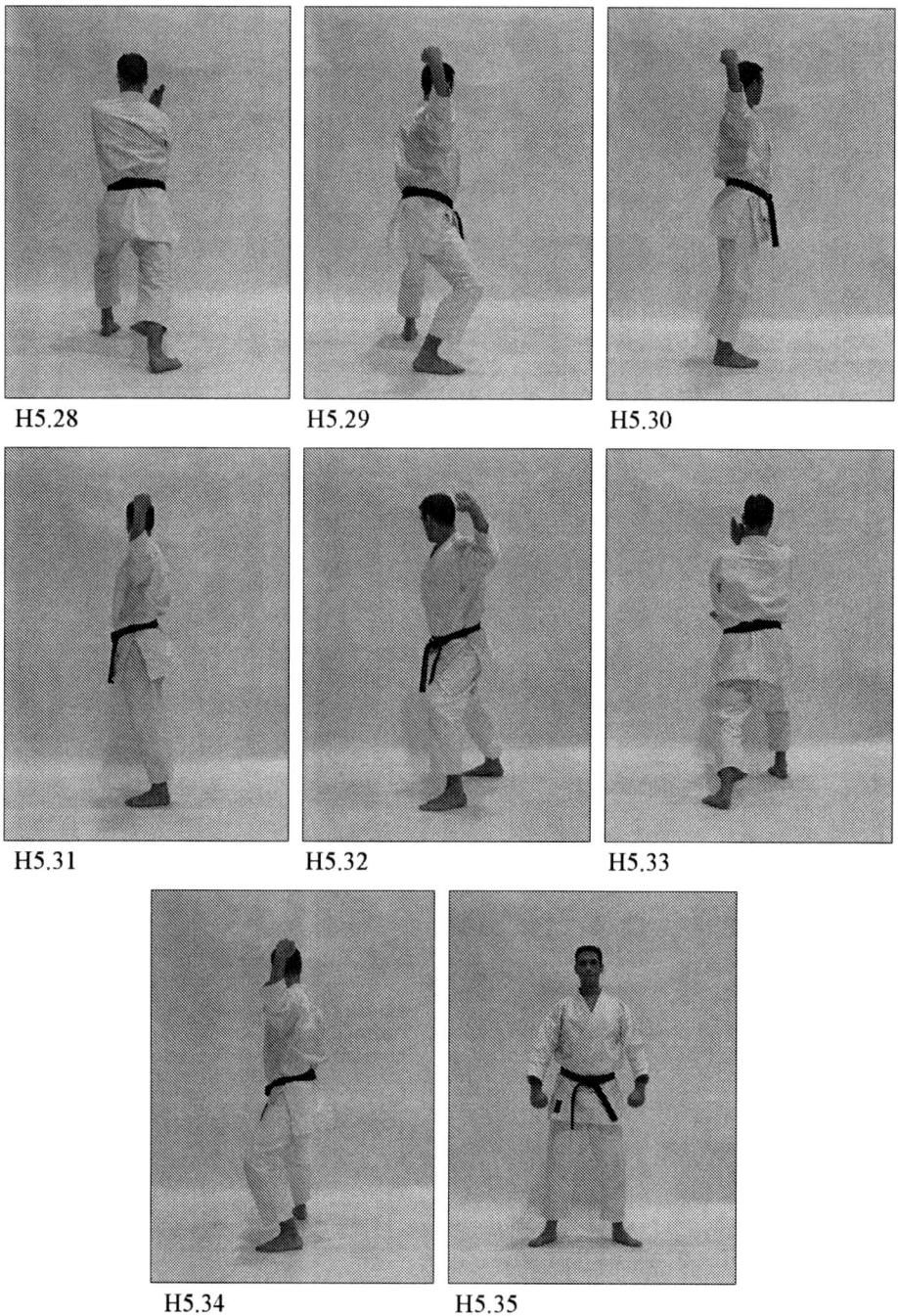

H5.28 H5.29 H5.30
H5.31 H5.32 H5.33
H5.34 H5.35

Training rationale

Please note that all drills should be practiced on both sides, however students should give prominence to defending from their habitual fence. To ensure a level of realism and technique flow, when struck practitioners are asked to simulate a 50-70% successful blow, thus folding over in response to punches or head strikes but not dropping completely as per a knockout. This allows students to train to follow through naturally from one technique into another with a more realistic body position that is not provided by a purely rigid training partner. In many instances these people make a remarkable recovery midway through the drills, but this serves to keep both practitioners on their toes. The simulation of the body's reaction to actual strikes also teaches students about how the body is likely to move, serves as mental preparation for real events and improves visualisation skills.

The Godan drills supplement the core of self defence applications provided by the preceding drills in two ways; firstly by providing alternative methods of applying previously learnt techniques with alternative redundancy patterns, and secondly by introducing new techniques to negate alternative HAOV.

The purpose of the Heian Godan drills is as follows:

- To provide students with alternative pre-emptive striking methods with multiple redundancy patterns that can be used in a free flowing situation.
- To introduce new HAOV and appropriate counter-measures.
- To increase the element of unpredictability in paired training.

Changes to the kata movement in the Heian Flow System

Sequences of movements are either initiated from a fence or a middle or end game fighting position instead of/ in addition to the preceding movement in the Kata. Some sequences begin from movements found in previous stages in the Heian set.

The line of movement at the start of the Kata varies although the arm movements are essentially the same.

The cross legged stance has not been retained in applications against standing attackers since it provides less stability than other stances available. The cross legged position is utilised however when the same finishing position is demonstrated with the attacker prone on the ground.

The jumping technique in this Kata has been replaced by a similar ground based movement that throws an attacker.

Heian Godan drills

Drill 33

White faces Blue and takes hold of both his biceps (Pic 5.33.1). Blue pivots in a clockwise fashion, pulling his right arm back and extending his left arm forwards to backfist across and down onto White's left temple while striking down onto White's left biceps with his right knuckles (Pic 5.33.2).

Pic 5.33.1   Pic 5.33.2
                         (H5.3)

Variation 1. White has not let go of Blue's right arm. Blue's right hand grips White's left sleeve just behind the elbow and rolls over the top in a counter-clockwise direction as he pivots his body in the same direction (Pic 5.33.3). Blue then pivots clockwise while maintaining downward pressure on White's arm and strikes to his face with a left roundhouse elbow strike (Pic 5.33.4). If this has still not dropped White then Blue can step forward with his left leg into White, striking White's temple with a left inside receiver while his right fist punches into White's ribs (Pic 5.33.5).

Heian Godan

Pic 5.33.3 (H5.4)   Pic 5.33.4 (H5.5)   Pic 5.33.5 (H5.10)

Variation 2. White has let go of Blue's right arm. Blue strikes into White's right ribs/triceps with an uppercut (or elbow strike if closer)(Pic 5.33.6). Blue then pivots clockwise to strike into White's neck with a left hook (Pic 5.33.7) before wrapping his left arm round White's neck in a headlock (Pic 5.33.8). White can then escape from the headlock as per Drill 19.

Pic 5.33.6 (H5.4)   Pic 5.33.7 (H5.5)   Pic 5.33.8 (H5.5)

Effectiveness	Comment
HAOV	The double grab (or push) followed by a head butt is one of the most common forms of attack recorded. In this drill the stimulus is merely a grab, but in either case defensive movement should be initiated before any other form of attack can be initiated.
Multiplicity	The techniques used in this drill can be used alternatively in response to a single arm grab (with A's left fist attacking to the bridge of the nose or neck rather than the bicep) or, in the case of variation 2, pre-emptively in a non-contact close proximity situation. The attack can also be used in close proximity in a mid game situation.
Predictable Response	This drill exploits the predictable movement of the body following manipulation of the arm at the back of the elbow.
Initiative	This drill initiates from a position of disadvantage and regains the initiative through avoiding a potential initial aggressive strike with a pre-emptive series of attacks.
Redundancy	The drill uses multiple strikes so that if the initial strike fails the defender is trained to follow through without pause thus reducing the chance of losing the initiative. The side step further reduces the chances of any initial blow landing.
Vital Points	Potential strikes to HT 2, ST 5, mind point, ear, ST 9, CO 18, ST 12, LV 13.
Unbalancing	Potential unbalancing from above due to strikes to ear.

Effectiveness	Comment
Adrenaline Tolerant	Moderate. Works with the natural reflex to move away, but without sufficient drilling some practitioners may freeze involuntarily when grabbed by both arms. Uses simple motor skills.
Low Maintenance	Yes.
Transferable skills	Works basic punching, striking, headlocking and stepping skills that can be employed in other drills.

Drill 34

Opposite push:

White pushes Blue's right shoulder with his left hand (Pic 5.34.1). Blue moves his right shoulder and twists to absorb the energy of the push and simultaneously with his left fist inside White's arms backfist strikes the top of White's left temple (Pic 5.34.2). Blue pulls on White's head as he punches with his right fist (Pic 5.34.3). As White buckles slightly, Blue follows through by pivoting clockwise with a left roundhouse elbow strike (Pic 5.34.4). Blue then steps forwards striking to White's left temple with a left inside receiver as he punches into White's ribs with his right fist (Pic 5.34.5).

Pic 5.34.1

Pic 5.34.2
(H5.3)

Pic 5.34.3
(H5.4)

Heian Godan

Pic 5.34.4
(H5.5)

Pic 5.34.5
(H5.10)

Effectiveness	**Comment**
HAOV	A push is one of the most common forms of attack recorded. In this drill the stimulus is merely a push but the expected attack would probably be a push/punch combination which is why in this drill the defender steps back and slight to the right so as to move further offline from the anticipated punch.
Multiplicity	The techniques used in this drill can be used alternatively as shown in Drill 33 or pre-emptively in a non-contact close proximity situation. The attack can also be used in close proximity in a mid game situation.
Predictable Response	This drill exploits the predictable movement of the body following strikes to the ribcage/abdomen and pulling on the arm.

Effectiveness	Comment
Initiative	This drill initiates from a position of disadvantage and regains the initiative through avoiding a potential initial aggressive strike with a pre-emptive series of attacks.
Redundancy	The drill uses multiple strikes so that if the initial strike fails the defender is trained to follow through without pause thus reducing the chance of losing the initiative. The side step further reduces the chances of any initial blow landing. The actual movement of the initial left hand strike can also be used to block a punch if need be, in which case the drill continues as normal with a follow through punch.
Vital Points	Potential strikes to HT 2, ST 5, mind point, ear, ST 9, CO 18, ST 12, LV 13, LU 7, SP 10, strangle.
Unbalancing	Potential unbalancing from above due to strikes to ear, pulling on LU 7. Potential unbalancing from below if strangle step connects with SP 10.
Adrenaline Tolerant	Yes. Uses simple movements to good effect. With the training in prior drills giving familiarity with being pushed, there should be little adverse reaction to stall either mind or body.
Low Maintenance	Yes.
Transferable skills	Works basic punching, striking, strangling and stepping skills that have been rehearsed in many previous drills.

Drill 35

White takes hold of Blue's left lapel (as per Drill 18) (Pic 5.35.1).

Pic 5.35.1

Blue steps forward into White with a left inside receiver to White's temple and a right punch to White's ribs (Pic 5.35.2). Blue then strikes down onto White's bicep with his left fist (Pic 5.35.3) and attempts to push White back with an elbow push to White's sternum (Pic 5.35.4).

Pic 5.35.2　　　　　　　Pic 5.35.3　　　　　　　Pic 5.35.4
(H3.11)　　　　　　　　(H3.12)　　　　　　　　(H3.12)

In the following scenario Blue progresses through a series of possible strikes, moving automatically from one to another as if each has been unsuccessful. Blue's actions here depend upon White's responses – White can choose to fall or stand with each part of the sequence – forcing Blue to continue his attack if need be. Usually this drill is done with White attempting to counter strangle, grab, push or pull on Blue's arms, forcing Blue to switch tactics, this has been omitted from the photographs to allow greater clarity.

Blue shifts his left fist down to downsweep into the left hand side of White's abdomen (Pic 5.35.5). Blue then punches over the top of this arm into the right hand side of White's abdomen (Pic 5.35.6).

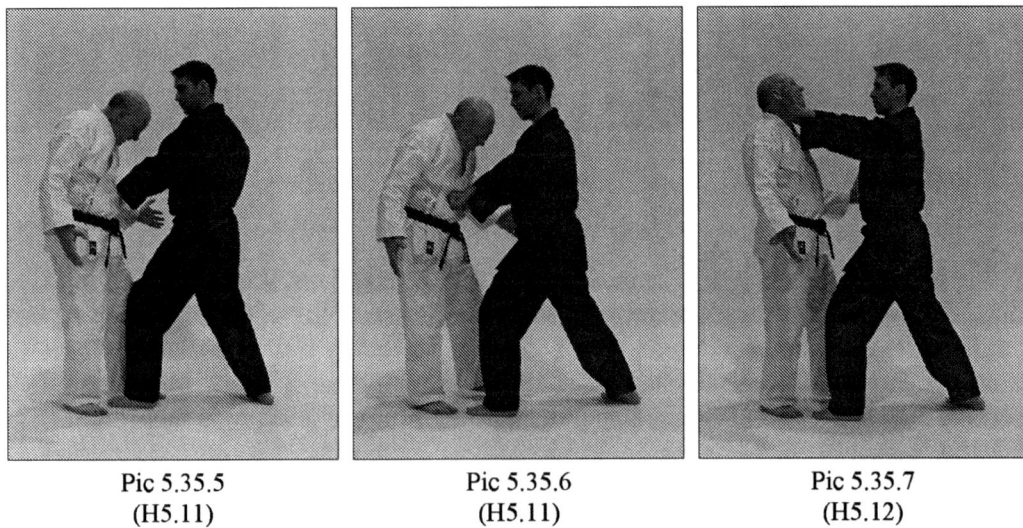

Pic 5.35.5
(H5.11)

Pic 5.35.6
(H5.11)

Pic 5.35.7
(H5.12)

Blue thrusts both hands upwards to strike simultaneously with the blades of both hands into both sides of White's neck (Pic 5.35.7).

Blue drops both hands slightly and allows his right hand to grasp White's left lapel (alternatively the crook of the thumb and wrist can be driven into the neck tissue). Blue then rings his left hand under and over his right to push into the right hand side of White's jaw as he simultaneously pulls with his right hand, strangling White (Pic 5.35.8).

Pic 5.35.8 (H5.13 & H5.14)   Pic 5.35.9 (H5.15)   Pic 5.35.10 (H5.16)

With the failure of the strangle Blue punches into the left hollow of White's shoulder (LU 1) with his right fist as he takes grabs and pulls White's right arm with his left hand, stepping with his right leg to the outside of White (Pic 5.35.9). Blue then pivots in a counter clockwise fashion and throws White over his hip (Pic 5.35.10). Having thrown White, Blue continues to step in the direction of his pivot and stamps down onto White with his right foot (Pic 5.35.11 and 5.35.12).

Pic 5.35.11 (H5.16)   Pic 5.35.12 (H5.17)

Alternatively Blue cannot throw White (either through deliberate choice or through White's resistance) and thus retracts his extended right arm before striking into White's right kidney with a right downsweep without shifting position (Pic 5.35.13). Blue then wraps his right arm round White's abdomen and steps forward behind White with his left leg, kneeing his Coccyx (Pic 5.35.14) and striking White's spine just above the shoulder blades with a left elbow strike (Pic 5.35.15).

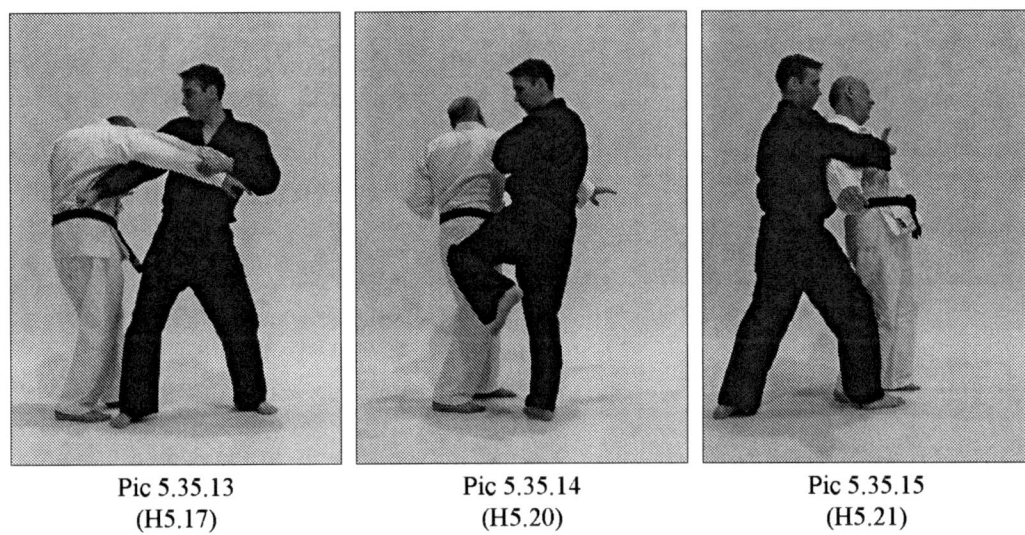

Pic 5.35.13
(H5.17)

Pic 5.35.14
(H5.20)

Pic 5.35.15
(H5.21)

Blue takes hold of White's left lapel with his right arm and then punches up into the base of White's skull with his right hand before applying pressure with his left arm against the right hand side of White's neck to create a strangle (Pic 5.35.16).

Pic 5.35.16
(H5.22 &H5.23)

Effectiveness	Comment
HAOV	A one handed front clothing grab followed by a punch to the head is one of the most commonly recorded attacks.
Multiplicity	Many of the techniques shown here could be used pre-emptively or in other mid game situations.
Predictable Response	This drill exploits the predictable movement of the body following particular strikes whether they be fully successful or not.
Initiative	This drill scores highly since although it responds to a grab, it is proactive in not waiting for any subsequent percussive technique. Once the drill begins it maintains the initiative with a flurry of strikes to multiple targets at different levels to confuse, disorientate and disable the attacker. The techniques of this drill may also be used proactively without waiting for any lapel grab.
Redundancy	The opening technique consists of two strikes so that in the unlikely event that one is deflected, the other is likely to hit its own target and thus buy the time to move through with the next strike. The multiple strikes drilled ensure that if anything fails at one level there is an automatic follow up. This entire drill is a rehearsal of redundancies for redundancies with the onus laid on White to challenge Blue at any point in time through non compliance, teaching Blue when to abandon one line of attack for another in order to keep the initiative and not lose an advantage. This drill is of course heavily linked to Drills 18 and its many other redundancies which share elements that may interact and overlap.

Effectiveness	Comment
Vital Points	Potential strikes to SP 10, LU 7, LR 13, LR 14, SP 10, GB 1, GB 2, mind point, ST3, SI 17, CO 18, LU 5, Bicep, CV 14, ST 9, ST 5, ear, LU 1, BL 57.
Unbalancing	Potential unbalancing from above due to strikes to ear, pulling on LU 7. Potential unbalancing from below if strangle step connects with SP 10. Sweeping technique.
Adrenaline Tolerant	Yes. Uses simple movements to good effect. With the training in prior drills giving familiarity there should be little adverse reaction to stall either mind or body. The strangulation technique may be the hardest to do under stressful conditions – but the same hand movement may be performed high speed as an effective head strike.
Low Maintenance	Yes.
Transferable skills	Works basic punching, striking, strangling and stepping skills that have been rehearsed in many previous drills.

Drill 36

White grabs hold of Blue's extended left arm with his right hand (as in Drills 20 and its redundancies) (Pic 5.36.1).

Pic 5.36.1
(H3.15)

Blue steps into White with his right leg, crescent kicking to White's leg at Sp 10 (or SP 7) (Pic 5.36.2) and striking either White's chest or jaw with his right elbow (if White's head has dropped with the leg strike) (Pic 5.36.3). Blue maintains hold of White's right arm with his left hand and extends his own right arm up through White's right armpit (Pic 5.36.4).

Pic 5.36.2   Pic 5.36.3   Pic 5.36.4
(H5.20)   (H5.21)   (H5.22)

Blue then pivots in a counter-clockwise direction, bringing both arms down in front of him and throwing White over his hip, keeping hold of White's right arm with his left hand (Pic 5.36.5 and Pic 5.36.6).

If White attempts to rise, Blue should drop his right knee directly onto White's head and apply pressure to his temple through his body weight with his hands poised to strike (Pic 5.36.7).

Pic 5.36.5
(H5.24 - H5.25)

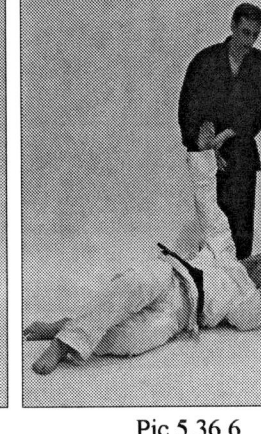
Pic 5.36.6
(H5.25)

Pic 5.36.7
(H5.25)

Effectiveness	Comment
HAOV	A one handed front clothing grab followed by a punch to the head is one of the most commonly recorded attacks. This HAOV can lead to this position but alternatively a simple arm grab could be the trigger for this technique.
Multiplicity	The techniques used in this drill can be used either reactively or proactively. The attack can also be used in close proximity or medium in a mid game situation without an arm grab as a low level initiated attack.
Predictable Response	This drill exploits the predictable movement of the body following particular strikes whether they be fully successful or not.

Effectiveness	Comment
Initiative	This drill scores highly since although it responds to a grab, it is proactive in not waiting for any subsequent percussive technique. Once the drill begins it maintains the initiative with multiple level strikes and a throw to confuse, disorientate and disable the attacker. The techniques of this drill may also be used proactively without waiting for any grab.
Redundancy	The opening technique consists of a low level strike that is difficult to anticipate in a real situation. As an alternative to the throw Blue could simply move into Drill 18 and apply a right inside receiver immediately following the elbow strike.
Vital Points	Potential strikes to SP 10, SP 7, ST 5, ST 3, mind point, GB 2, GB 1. Ear, strangle.
Unbalancing	Potential unbalancing from above due to strikes to ear and the throw. Potential unbalancing from below from kick to either SP 10 or SP 7.
Adrenaline Tolerant	Yes. Uses simple movements to good effect.
Low Maintenance	Yes.
Transferable skills	Works kicking and striking kills that are found in other Kata such as Bassai Dai.

Drill 37

Blue and White face each other at close range (Pic 5.37.1).

Pic 5.37.1

White lunges low with both arms to tackle Blue's waist and A strikes upwards with his right hand into White's sternum as his left hand slaps the back of White's neck (GB20) (Pic 5.37.2).

Pic 5.37.2 Pic 5.37.3
(H5.28) (H5.29)

Blue pulls his right arm back and up, keeping it bent as if for a bicep curl, trapping White's left arm tightly between his ribs and his arm and applying pressure to White's elbow. As White twists with the pressure of Blue's right arm movement Blue retracts his left hand further towards the side of his head in a preliminary down sweep movement, striking the right hand side of White's head with his left elbow. Blue then follows this by down sweeping with his left arm, striking the other side of White's head with his elbow (Pic 5.37.3). This technique will only work if the right arm is inside the lunge, otherwise the diver's left arm will prevent it from reaching the sternum (which is what prevents you from going to the ground in this instance). This technique is unlikely to work on a professional grappler and is aimed towards an unskilled rugby tackle from an inebriated assailant.

Effectiveness	**Comment**
HAOV	Although this attack has not made the official statistics, such lunges have been seen on CCTV footage. They either initiate a fight with one person trying to take the other to the ground, or they form a mid-game attack response when one of the attackers is either trying to avoid strikes or is too tired/drunk to exchange percussive blows.
Multiplicity	The techniques used in this drill can be also be employed in an alternative defence outlined in Drill 38.
Predictable Response	This drill exploits the predictable movement of the body following a sternum strike.
Initiative	This drill scores poorly since it is purely reactive to the potential danger of being taken to the ground.
Redundancy	If the initial strikes should fail to drop the attacker there is a built in redundancy of the rough arm pin and double strikes to the head. The strikes can of course be employed without using the arm pin and there is no reason why the defender should not take advantage of the position of his knees to strike from below as well as above, moving into Drill 28.
Vital Points	Potential strikes to CV 14, GB 20, GB 1, mind point, ear.

Effectiveness	Comment
Unbalancing	Potential unbalancing from above due to strikes to ear and sternum.
Adrenaline Tolerant	Yes. Uses simple movements to good effect and requires no specialised footwork.
Low Maintenance	Yes.
Transferable skills	Uses and reinforces the motor responses for the common technique of Down Sweep.

Drill 38
Variation 1:

Blue faces White in a left fence (Pic 5.38.1).

Pic 5.38.1

White crosses with his right hand. Blue shifts to the side of the cross, palming aside with his left hand as he slides deeply forward, attacking White's ribs with his left elbow as his right hand slaps upwards into White's genitals (Pic 5.38.2). Blue then pushes his left hand down hard on the left hand side of White's neck as he lifts White's left leg with his right hand (Pic 5.38.3), dropping White to the ground (Pic 5.38.4).

| Pic 5.38.2 | Pic 5.38.3 | Pic 5.38.4 |
| (H5.28) | (H5.29) | (H5.29) |

Variation 2:

Blue faces White in a left fence (Pic 5.38.5).

White throws a left hook at Blue which Blue deflects with his left hand, driving his body low into White and slapping White's groin with his right hand (Pic 5.38.6) . Blue then pushes his left arm down underneath White's armpit and raises White's left leg with his right hand, throwing White (Pic 5.38.7).

| Pic 5.38.5 | Pic 5.38.6 | Pic 5.38.7 |
| | (H5.28) | (H5.29) |

Effectiveness	Comment
HAOV	A swinging punch is one of the most commonly recorded HAOV.
Multiplicity	The techniques used in this drill can be also be employed in an alternative defence outlined in Drill 37.
Predictable Response	This drill exploits the predictable movement of the body following a strike to the genitals.
Initiative	This drill is reactive, but can also be used proactively at close range with a slapping attack to GB 20 or the ear instead of a parry.
Redundancy	If the strike to the groin fails to have effect then the defender is still in a good position to change tactics (for example the elbow strike to the kidneys and knee strike to the coccyx at the end of Drill 31). The throw should not be attempted unless the attacker is clearly incapacitated.
Vital Points	Potential strikes to GB 20, ear, genitalia, SP 10.
Unbalancing	Potential unbalancing from above due to strikes to ear and from below due to the genitalia strike and throw.
Adrenaline Tolerant	Yes. Uses simple movements to good effect and requires no specialised footwork.
Low Maintenance	The initial parry is low maintenance but the throw requires a degree of regular practice.
Transferable skills	Uses and reinforces the motor responses for the common technique of Down Sweep.

Advanced points

By this time students should be looking to strike and grab available vital points in the target areas indicated. Wherever possible steps to both the inside and outside leg should attack points at those points.

Whenever a partner is dropped to the ground, students should be looking to see if they are able to apply one of the controlling techniques illustrated in any of the parts of the Heian Flow System.

Once these alternative drills have been learnt, students should be able to able to vary at will according to their preferences the techniques they chose to use within Flow System training. As a result of this training becomes less predictable and students are forced to learn to watch for subtle shifts in movement that may indicate the lines of attack and defence pursued.

Vital Point References

These works are recommended study for readers interested in vital point anatomy.

Erle Montague, *The Encyclopedia of Dim-Mak, Main Meridians,* Paladin US, 1997.

Erle Montague, *The Encylopedia of Dim-Mak, Extra Meridians, Points and More,* Paladin US 1997.

Mark Tedeschi, *Essential Anatomy for Martial and Healing Arts*, Weatherhill Inc, 2000.

Lightning Source UK Ltd.
Milton Keynes UK
12 April 2011

170789UK00004B/34/A